Talking
About
Mime

Talking About Mime

An Illustrated Guide

David Alberts

Photographs by J. J. McClintock

HEINEMANN
Portsmouth, NH

Heinemann
A division of Reed Elsevier Inc.
361 Hanover Street
Portsmouth, NH 03801–3912

Offices and agents throughout the world

Library of Congress Cataloging-in-Publication Data

Alberts, David.
    Talking about mime : an illustrated guide / David Alberts ; photographs by J. J. McClintock.
       p.   cm.
    Includes bibliographical references.
    ISBN 0–435–08641–3
    1. Mime. I. Title.
PN2071.G4A4   1994
792.3—dc20   94–18094
                                            CIP

Editor: Lisa A. Barnett
Production: Vicki Kasabian
Cover design: Catherine Hawkes
Cover photograph: Cheryl Kimball

Printed in the United States of America on acid-free paper
98 97 96 95 94 EB 1 2 3 4 5

Contents

Illusions and Exercises

Preface

The life of an artist is a strange one, filled with triumphs and tragedies, some of our own making, others predestined, it seems, and unavoidable. In mime, the product of our sometimes considerable efforts is ephemeral, often insubstantial, and occasionally inconsequential. Painters have their paintings, writers their books, but of acting, dance, mime, and all the other live-and-in-person arts, there remains only a memory. Our endeavors exist, and can *only* exist, through us, the performers, and only for the moment. We accept that. The material rewards are also few, and, for the most part, insignificant. The true rewards are reflected in the eyes of the audience and in the minds and bodies of our dedicated students. The joy of our endeavors lies in the work itself, with the people whose lives we have touched, and with those who have touched our lives in return.

I would like to extend my heartfelt thanks and appreciation to a number of people for their guidance and support in the preparation and writing of this book. To my teacher, mentor, and friend, Dr. Nancy Wynn Zucchero, whose memory sustains my lifelong devotion to the art of mime; to Dr. Allen Kepke and K. Leslie; to my family and friends, particularly my daughters Morgan, Sarah, and Samantha; to all the fine actors, directors, mimes, dancers, designers, and technicians with whom I've had the privilege of working through the years; and especially to my students, past, present, and yet to be. To all, many thanks.

Introduction

*W*hat is mime? What is so unique about it? What makes mime truly different from all other performing arts?

There is no simple, twenty-five-words-or-less definition that fully explains all that mime is. How can you describe in words an art that uses no words? Mime shares many characteristics with the other performing arts, but it has certain unmistakable characteristics of its own that help define it more clearly.

First of all, mime is an *art,* an original and independent performing art. It is a means of self-expression, of conveying thoughts, ideas, feelings, and perceptions about a performing artist's environment to an audience. It is the selective interpretation and representation of the artist's concept of life or of one particular aspect of it. The *art* of mime is the *new* and *unique* experience that the performer and audience share in performance. The personal artistry of mime is in the sense of "new life" that the mime artist brings to a performance, a sense of doing something for the first time even though it may have been rehearsed and performed countless times before.

Mime, as an art, is also a form of *communication*. This communication is the continuous exchange of ideas, thoughts, images, and emotions between the performer and the audience. The communication flows from the performer to the audience and back again in a continuous, unbroken cycle. It is a bond between the performer and the audience, an experience in which they share equally.

Mime is *movement* that expresses thought. The thought may be simple or complex, and the movement symbolic or prosaic, but the thought and movement are entirely and completely interdependent. In its pure form, mime is expressed *only* through the movement and gestures of the body. This movement is a physical expression of an idea, a thought, or a feeling that the performer wishes to convey to the audience. The audience will not comprehend even the simplest thought without some physical representation of it, nor will an audience understand seemingly random, uncontrolled movement without a corresponding and underlying thought process. There must be some context in which the thought is expressed, and that context is the movement of the body.

There is a clear and specific meaning held within each movement and gesture. An audience perceives and understands what these movements and gestures mean directly and intuitively, without explanation or verbal translation. The physical image of the performer, the performer's movement, and what the performer wishes to express are all linked together in the mind of the audience in one single form of expression.

Mime is *silent*—by choice and by design. Mime is free of the often confusing, inconsistent, arbitrary, and ambiguous elements of spoken or written language. It is not a guessing game, "charades," which is a language-based activity. The art of mime is universal, understood by people throughout the world, no matter what language they speak. Mime and words can complement each other, of course, but on the purest level, if it is necessary to speak or give written explication, it is not necessary to mime. Communication in mime exists beyond written and spoken language. In mime, there is only "show"—no "tell."

Mime is physical *illusion*. Until the 1920s, the physical illusions of mime as we know them—walking against the wind, tug-of-war, and the wall, for example—simply did not exist. These illusions, and others, were first devised by Étienne Decroux in the 1920s and 1930s, as exercises that actors could use to help them learn to control their bodies. With the help of Jean-Louis Barrault, Decroux later developed these exercises into a new and completely different art form, the art of modern mime. No art form other than mime is based in these physical illusions. Any other performing art, such as acting or dance, that uses physical illusion in training or performance is itself relying on the art of mime, as it was originally created and developed by Decroux.

Physical illusion in mime is based on three underlying principles: *counterweight, foreshortening,* and *attitude.* Counterweight is the technique of *muscular compensation* for an imaginary force or an imaginary object. In the illusion of tug-of-war, for example, the performer shows the force exerted on the rope by reacting to, or *countering,* that force, by pulling against it. In showing an imaginary object, the performer reacts physically to the imagined size, weight, and shape of the object in order to define that object for the audience.

Foreshortening is a *condensation* of an action. In mime, an action, such as walking, is closely analyzed in order to determine the *essential* physical elements of the movement—what it is that makes walking look like walking. These essential elements are then combined and *condensed* in time and space. The resulting illusion *looks* like walking but is not exactly the same movement as real walking, and the performer doesn't actually *go* anywhere.

Attitude is the *manner* in which an illusion (or any other action in mime) is performed. The speed, rhythm, and intensity of a movement conveys to the audience a mood or an emotional context for the illusion. Smooth, flowing movements express an entirely different feeling than short, staccato movements and impart a different meaning to the performer's actions. "Walking" at a slow, deliberate pace, with head down and hands hanging limply at the sides denotes a completely different feeling than the very same illusion performed with a sprightly, bouncing gait, arms swinging, and head held high. This principle of attitude applies equally to any movement in mime.

Mime involves the creative manipulation and control of *time, space,* and *energy.* Time is the dimension of the relationship between *experiences.* Time is relative to the performer's definition or use of it. A mime performer can show the passage of a few seconds or of a lifetime with a simple gesture. Space is the dimension of the relationship between *things,* real or imaginary. The mime can define space through simple illusions to show the universe or only a small part of it. In mime, energy is *motion,* motion is change, and change is constant. The mime performer perceives the environment as a continually changing medium of experience, not simply as a massive collection of people, objects, and momentary, disassociated occurrences. Because time, space, and energy are limitless, there is virtually no limit either to what a mime performer can do. A mime is not bounded by the space in which she works, for instance, simply because the performer can reinvent the space to suit her performance. Through the control of his own physical energy, the performer can make the most difficult activity seem simple and easy and make the simplest activity appear to be incredibly difficult. The possibilities for expression in mime are limited only by the limits of the performer's imagination.

Mime is *imagination.* The human mind cannot distinguish between *reality* and what is *imagined* as reality. This is the principle on which acting techniques such as "sense memory" and "emotional memory" are based. We "feel" what we *imagine* we feel. Through physical illusions, mime makes the imaginary seem real. An audience fills in the blanks in a performance with its imagination. The audience "sees" what is not actually there, and actually *believes* what it "sees." An essential element of mime is this *imaginative response* of the audience. The audience must be considered an active participant in the mime performance.

It is a common misconception that mime is based solely or primarily in imagination—that the best mime performer is necessarily the most imaginative one. On the contrary, mime is firmly based in *reality.* The mime performer draws raw material from reality, from the surrounding world, and uses that reality to lead the audience into an imagined world. An audience member who has never seen another person eating an apple or blowing up a balloon or simply walking down the street would have great difficulty relating to any mime performance that utilized those activities. There would be no frame of reference for that person, and the illusions would make no sense.

The mime performer must possess a keen awareness and understanding of the reality of the world. He or she must be knowledgeable in many, many things—music, dance, theatre, art, world literature, psychology, sociology, philosophy, cultural and ethnic diversities, anatomy, physics, the physical sciences, and occupations and the tools used in them, among other things—and be able to express these many things effectively in movement. The mime performer who best understands reality and who can best transform that reality into imagination will be the most successful mime. Reality comes first. The imaginative flights of creative fancy flow from there.

Mime involves both *technique* and artistic *expression.* Expression is *mental and emotional* and encompasses any of the ideas, thoughts, and/or feelings that the performer wishes to communicate to the audience. Technique is *physical*—the means by which the performer expresses ideas, thoughts, and feelings through the precise control and manipulation of the body. These two elements of technique and expression work very closely together. The expressive inner quality is achieved through technique—the organization and articulation of the work. A mime must not only know what it is she wishes to express, but also must be *able* to express it physically. Technique—what a performer *does*—and expression—what a performer *means*—must appear to the audience as one unified experience. To communicate effectively in mime, the performer must know, understand, and be able to *control* what his body is doing.

The three most distinguishing and unique characteristics of modern mime are (1) that it was *purposefully created* and developed by Étienne Decroux as a distinct and separate art form, (2) that it utilizes *physical illusion* in training and performance, and (3) that it relies on the *imaginative response of the audience* for its existence. No other performing art encompasses these three basic elements, and without them, there is no mime.

This book was written to help you learn the basic physical technique of the silent art of mime and to help you understand the expressive potential of the art. The short history of mime in Chapter 1 acquaints you with mime tradition and famous mime performers.

Chapters 2 through 6 focus on the basic exercises for the *face,* the *hands,* and the *feet.* These are the three centers of the body in the physical performance of mime. On the most basic level, your face tells the audience what you are thinking and feeling—your emotional involvement in the scene. Your hands define your environment—your imaginary props, costumes, and scenery. Your feet tell the audience where you are in relation to your imaginary environment. The solo and group exercises in these chapters will help you explore and develop your own mime pieces. These chapters also include scenarios for performance pieces based on the skills you have learned.

To help you apply these skills in performance, Chapter 7 explores characterization, Chapter 8 discusses the role of improvisation in developing original material, and Chapter 9 introduces the basics of mime makeup, costumes, lights, and so on, and how to apply all that you have learned in actual performance.

This book can be used with or without a teacher. There is no substitute for a good teacher, of course, but if you are unable to work with a teacher, you will still be able to teach yourself the basics of mime. If you prefer to study mime with friends, you will find you will readily encourage one another and will learn a great deal from one another as well. Alone, with a teacher, or with friends, this book will provide you with all you need to know to get started. With a little time and effort, you can learn the basics of mime, and you will soon be performing your own original mime pieces.

A Brief History of Mime

T he true origins of the art of mime have been obscured by the passage of time. Scholars have determined, however, that the first clear references to mimelike performances can be found in ancient Greece around the sixth century B.C. By the time of the first official drama festival in Athens in 534 B.C. (generally considered the beginning of our Western theatre tradition), the performance of mime had already been firmly established. Mime plays of the Greek classical period consisted of short, comic scenes based on everyday life, frequently dealt with topical issues, and often contained political satire. The mime plays were performed in the streets and in other outdoor performance areas, and were often used as short introductory scenes before many of the performances of the Greek classic plays. As an introductory scene, the mime play was used to teach a moral lesson to the audience based on the theme of the play that was to follow.

The popular form of Greek mime was more an entertainment or an amusement than a full-fledged dramatic presentation. The mime performance was usually improvised along a well-known story line. It was accompanied by music, song, and dance and very often included acrobatics and juggling as part of the entertainment. Full-face masks were also used by the mime performers, usually for the stock characters such as the miserly old man, the foolish doctor or lawyer, the comic servant, and so on.

By 300 B.C., mime performances were an accepted part of the official theatre festivals in Greece. Aristotle mentions mime in his description of the plays of his time. He noted, for instance, that in the performance of these mime plays, many gestures and movements were used, particularly by the *Chorus,* the narrators of the plays. Unlike modern mimes, however, these early mime performers were quite talkative. The mime actors also used realistic props and performed in a highly stylized, exaggerated, and what was considered by some to be an "undignified" manner. The performers' movements were very broad, and their costumes were exaggerated as well. Incidentally, although *all* the actors in the regular Greek plays were men, the mime performances often included women.

Greek mime was total theatre. It utilized all the many skills of the performers in acting, dancing, singing, mime, juggling, and acrobatics, in a popular and *accessible* theatrical form. It was varied, direct, immediate, and topical.

Roman mime essentially evolved from Greek mime. The Romans simply adapted the Greek mime to their own culture and to their own theatrical tradition. Roman mime was improvised, like the earlier Greek mime, and also used music, song, dance, narration, and masks. The use of masks in Roman mime gradually decreased over time, which naturally increased the emphasis on facial expression. Like Greek mime, a performance of Roman mime was most often based on scenes from everyday life, included topical political satire, and used easily recognized stock characters. Mime was performed along with other popular entertainments of the time, including acrobatics, juggling, and other feats of physical skill (including the significantly more daring entertainments in the Coliseum).

There is a legend that Livius Andronicus, a Roman playwright and actor, was the first to perform mime in Rome. According to the legend, Livius lost his voice during the performance of one of his plays but (trouper that he was) continued to act his part without speaking while another actor provided the appropriate narration. This particular legend has been disproved by many theatre scholars, but it's a good story nevertheless.

Roman *pantomime,* as opposed to Roman *mime,* is a unique theatrical form that was introduced in the first century B.C. Roman pantomime was a clear departure from any previous form of theatrical presentation. It was a solo, silent interpretive or rhythmic dance performed to a spoken or sung narration. The pantomime performer wore a closed-mouth mask, which did not allow him to speak (the masks of Greek and Roman mime were open-mouthed and did permit speech), and often performed more than one character, changing masks and costumes to indicate the changes in character. It is likely that music accompanied the performance, which probably helped facilitate the character changes.

Roman pantomime is closely associated with our own concept of mime—a solo dancer/mime who performs various characters, often in a well-known story. Although the Roman pantomime employed narration in the presentation, the solo performer relied entirely on movement and gesture to convey the characters and the story.

The subjects of these pantomime performances were usually tales from Roman mythology and the heroic love stories of the Roman gods and goddesses. Unlike Roman *mime,* however, Roman *pantomime* was serious rather than comic and appealed more to the upper-class Romans than to the common people. Roman pantomime was most often performed in theatres or in private homes, not in the streets, and appealed to a fairly limited audience that included primarily the educated and the well-to-do. Mime and pantomime performances were occasionally attended by the emperors. (One emperor, Justinian, was so taken with a mime performer named Theodora that he married her.)

After the fall of Rome, the serious Roman *pantomime* was no longer performed. However, the more comic *mime* continued to be performed, although on a more limited scale, by traveling groups of performers. These itinerant players upheld the mime tradition for nearly a thousand years during the Middle Ages, from the sixth to the fifteenth centuries, by performing in village squares, streets, and marketplaces throughout Europe.

Mime evolved very little during the Middle Ages, but it appears to have been no less popular with the people than it had been with the Greeks and Romans. Few records remain of that time, but it is likely that mime was performed in the Middle Ages in the same improvised fashion it had been in Greek and Roman times, with comic scenes of daily life and political satire the usual subject matter. There were stock characters and masks, as well as acrobatics, juggling, music, song, and dance.

The single greatest influence on mime in Europe after the Middle Ages was the *commedia dell'arte,* an immensely popular form of Italian street theatre that evolved in the fifteenth century. *Commedia* troupes performed to enthusiastic audiences throughout Europe from the midfifteenth through the eighteenth centuries. The *commedia* is the most notable example in the history of theatre of the *spirit* of mime—its vitality, diversity, spontaneity, creativity, and widespread popularity.

The *commedia dell'arte* was basically an improvised form of theatre. Actors portrayed stock characters, most of whom (except for the young lovers) wore masks. (Some actors played the same stock character for their entire performing lives.) The performances were almost always comic, and were played according to a rough plot outline, or *scenario,* from which the actors improvised the play. The scenario was a brief description of the props, characters, entrances and exits, and basic overall action of the play. The rest was left to the actors' imagination. The performance likely included a short prologue and other standard, nonimprovised introductory speeches for the stock characters, but the major part of the play was improvised. The plays were most often based on the amorous adventures of the principal characters and were full of exaggerated movement and a great deal of broad physical activity, as well as music, acrobatics, and juggling. Early scenarios of the *commedia* were unsophisticated, but they were gradually developed and refined and were passed down from one performing troupe to another, generation to generation, for over two hundred years.

The influence of the *commedia* was most strongly felt in France. Traveling *commedia* troupes performed throughout France on a regular basis, sometimes touring the country for months at a time. By 1568, a few *commedia* troupes had decided to dispense with touring altogether and had settled permanently in Paris and in other cities. Molière's own company in Paris shared a theatre with a *commedia* troupe for several years, and the influence of the *commedia dell'arte* is apparent in many of Molière's plays. Many of his plots, scenes, intrigues, and characters are highly reminiscent of the *commedia*.

Gradually, however, the popularity of the Italian *commedia dell'arte* declined in France, and by the end of the eighteenth century, the *commedia* troupes had been replaced by popular French theatre companies, like the Comédie-Française, the most popular theatre company in Paris. The French theatre had gradually adopted many of the characters and characteristics of the *commedia,* adapted them to French culture, and amended them to fit within the French theatre tradition. Counterparts of many of the stock characters of the *commedia*, like Pantalone, Columbina, and Arlecchino, found their way into the French theatre. In contrast to the *commedia*, however, the French popular theatre was not improvised. The plays relied less on the juggling, acrobatics, and broad physical comedy that were the trademarks of the *commedia*. By the beginning of the nineteenth century, the emphasis in the French theatre was on traditional acting, characterization, and the spoken word.

One of the stock characters of the *commedia,* a comic servant named Pedrolino, was a favorite of French actors and audiences. Renamed *Pierrot* by Molière (in his play *Don Juan,* in 1665), this seemingly minor character of the *commedia* was to become a very important influence in the overall development of the art of mime. The character of Pierrot gradually evolved from a minor character (as it had been in the *commedia*) to a more important central character, and mime moved from the streets and village squares into the more important theatres in the heart of Paris. The character of Pierrot at this time was one of a gullible buffoon, a lazy fool who would rather eat than do anything else. Plays were written about Pierrot and his adventures in and out of love. People flocked to the theatres to enjoy his antics and revel in his amorous pursuits.

In time, the role of Pierrot fell to a young man named Jean-Gaspard Deburau (1796–1846), known as "Baptiste" for his innocent, unassuming demeanor. Jean-Gaspard was born into a theatrical family, but he was considered a fairly inept acrobat and a mediocre actor at best. It was by accident that young "Baptiste" came to portray Pierrot. In 1819, the leading actor suddenly left the theatre company performing at the Théâtre des Funambules in Paris, and with no one else to play the part, Jean-Gaspard was hastily fitted into the much-too-large costume and unceremoniously pushed onstage as Pierrot. For the art of mime, it was a very fortunate twist of fate.

Jean-Gaspard Deburau is the single most identifiable and important individual in the development of mime prior to the twentieth century. In whiteface, wearing a flowing white costume and saying not a word, Deburau quite simply reinvented the character of Pierrot. He changed Pierrot from a loutish, simpleminded, gluttonous fool to a subtle, refined, artistic, and expressive character with a broad intellectual and emotional range. So doing, Deburau single-handedly transformed Pierrot from a subservient role into a main character.

Deburau's characterization of Pierrot defined popular French pantomime in the mind of the general public. Deburau is considered the first true mime artist. He changed the form of mime from slapstick, as it had been in the *commedia,* into total theatre employing logical, clearly defined plots, well-developed characters, and topical references; mime was no longer simply traditional comic scenarios about the old stock characters. Deburau performed in over one hundred and fifty mime plays during his performing lifetime, and developed his own very distinguishable performance style. His Pierrot was a wistful and somewhat melancholy character, but one with a full range of emotions and physical abilities; he relied on skill and finesse rather than buffoonery.

Deburau was highly regarded as an actor and mime, and in spite of his own personal shortcomings (tried for murder in 1836, he was acquitted, due in part to his popularity), he had a considerable following throughout France. Deburau's genius lay in his versatility as a performer and in his ability to reach the hearts and minds of the theatre-going public through his performances as Pierrot.

Deburau continued to perform until his death in 1846. His son, Jean-Charles, carried on his father's legacy for a time, but after Deburau's death the public's interest in pantomime gradually diminished. The last performance at Deburau's theatre, the Théâtre des Funambules, on July 15, 1862, was a pantomime entitled *Memoires de Pierrot,* in which Jean-Charles played Pierrot. The performance is notable in that Jean-Charles played Pierrot not in his father's traditional white costume but in black. It was a fitting color. The day following the performance, the Funambules and six neighboring theatres were torn down to make way for the reconstruction of many of the streets and boulevards in the theatre district of Paris.

There was a resurgence of interest in pantomime—and in the character of Pierrot—in the 1880s. Paul Margueritte wrote and performed a pantomime entitled *Pierrot, Assassin de sa Femme* (*Pierrot, Assassin of His Wife*), in which Pierrot tickles his wife to death, and joined with others to form the Cercle Funambulesques, a performance group named after Deburau's theatre, the Théâtre des Funambules. The expressed purpose of the group was to revive the whiteface pantomime tradition of Deburau and to encourage the writing and performing of new plays and pantomimes written in the *commedia* style. The group disbanded after only fourteen performances, however, and the renewed interest in pantomime proved to be short-lived.

For a time, mime survived as an art form through occasional performances by individual performers and traveling mime troupes, but from the late 1800s until the 1920s, the art of mime was essentially forgotten. Mime was considered a secondary art form at best, and it was taught only as part of an actor's or dancer's movement training, as a physical training *technique,* rather than as an art form in its own right.

The concept of modern mime began in France in the early 1920s, in the experimental theatre school of Jacques Copeau in Paris. Copeau recognized the importance of mime in actor training. He believed that the evolution of expression in theatre begins with silence and movement, then moves to the spoken word. He incorporated mime technique into the school's curriculum, and the mask and movement exercises he taught were the first real emphasis on mime in any modern French acting school.

In 1923, Étienne Decroux, a twenty-five-year-old anarchist aspiring to a political career, entered Copeau's school to study rhetoric, hoping to improve his speaking skills. It is ironic that Decroux left Copeau's school a few years later having begun to build the foundation of a new and *silent* art, the art of modern mime.

While working with Copeau, Decroux studied improvisation, mask, and movement, but he soon became dissatisfied with the role mime was assigned in the school. Copeau used his training in mime only in support of the spoken word. Decroux felt that mime could stand on its own and that it deserved a much greater role in acting and in the performing arts in general. He envisioned a serious art form based on consistent principles of movement and gesture, and he intended to discover a method of training actors in this new art.

Decroux left Copeau's school and devoted the rest of his life to the development of the art of mime. At first, Decroux worked alone. In 1928, he organized a small group of actors to study mime, but the group disbanded soon thereafter, a result of Decroux's obsession with his art and the lack of popular support for their performances.

In 1931, Decroux met a promising young actor, Jean-Louis Barrault, who shared his enthusiasm for physical expression and the new art of mime. In the two years that they worked closely together, they forged the technical foundation of the art of mime. They explored and analyzed the principles of movement and gesture, and refined the basic physical technique of mime. With Barrault's help, Decroux stylized the expression of the body, and defined what he believed were the intellectual and emotional meanings of each physical action. They discovered, analyzed, and developed the basic mime exercises and physical illusions, such as walking and tug-of-war, that we know today.

Decroux and Barrault gradually developed differing philosophies of mime and in time parted company. Decroux continued to refine his new art and also acted in the Paris theatres, if only to support himself in his studies of mime. By 1941, Decroux felt he had refined his art sufficiently to open his own school of modern mime in Paris, in which he taught until his death in 1992, all the while seeking to improve and expand his art.

Barrault meanwhile embarked on his own distinguished career as an actor and director. One of Barrault's most famous acting roles was that of Jean-Gaspard Deburau in the 1946 film *Les Enfants du Paradis* (*Children of Paradise*), which premiered in Paris in the hundred-year anniversary of Deburau's death.

The art of mime that Decroux conceived was substantially different from the common perception of mime. Decroux shifted the emphasis from traditional comic entertainment to what he believed to be a more intellectually stimulating and artistically expressive form. He considered mime as a physical art form based on clearly defined principles of movement that could be taught and learned in the same way that any other art form is transferred from one person to another.

The modern popular concept of mime is based primarily on the style of one of Decroux's most prominent students, Marcel Marceau, who first came to the public's attention in the late 1940s. Marceau has done more than anyone else to establish the art of mime in this century. Marceau's performance style is firmly rooted in the classical French school of mime as approached through the philosophies and training of Decroux. Marceau's movements and gestures are fluid and stylized, and he relies heavily on the technical exercises and illusions of mime. His performances are primarily character studies, in which he uses all of the techniques of modern mime to establish his own complete theatrical environment—including set, props, and costume—all in silence. In some ways, Marceau's performances are a throwback to earlier forms of mime, particularly in his use of modern stock characters and scenes from daily life, reminiscent of Greek and Roman mime. Marceau has successfully bridged the gap between the ancient, historical forms of mime and its modern forms. His art is a synthesis of Greek mime, Roman pantomime, Italian *commedia,* and the French whiteface tradition of Deburau. His performance technique, however, is securely based in Decroux's principles of modern mime.

Marceau has performed throughout the world and has been seen by more people than any other theatrical mime performer in history. Marceau's influence on the development of mime has been considerable. In addition to his worldwide performances, he operates his own school of mime in Paris, where he has trained many young mime artists to carry on the tradition.

In the past few years, due in part to the influence of Marceau, there has been renewed interest in the study of mime. The art of mime is also being recognized as an important and essential part of an actor's training as well as a vital element of the performing arts. There have been some changes and stylistic developments in the art, however. Mime, like any other art form, is the product of the individual's unique perspective of life. The art of mime is embodied in its performing artists. Every mime artist approaches the art in his or her own way, drawing on both ancient and modern techniques and traditions to form a personal and *individual* art. Some mime performers have chosen to reject the traditional narrative form of mime in favor of a more abstract presentation style. Others have retained the narrative tradition but are performing without the whiteface, masks, or classically oriented costume. Whatever the presentation style, however, each is derived from the essential elements of modern mime as originally conceived and developed by Decroux—its purposeful creation, the use of physical illusions, and the responsive imagination of the audience.

The art of mime, in all its diverse forms, has endured and evolved through the centuries, from the early Greeks to the present day. Mime endures because it is not limited by considerations of geographical location, cultural orientation, or language. Mime endures because it appeals directly to the hearts and minds and souls of its audience. Mime endures most of all because it actively engages, stimulates, and expands the audience's imagination.

The Face 2

*F*acial expression is a vital element in the performance of mime. Without the animating qualities of the face, movement and gestures can often seem contrived, lacking feeling or expression. There are exceptions, of course. Silent-film star Buster Keaton was master of the "poker face." His eyes told the story for the rest of his face, and he was able to express the emotional context of his performance solely with his body. For the most part, however, mime performers rely on the face *and* body working together to tell the story.

There are five basic facial expressions in mime: happiness, sadness, surprise, anger, and fear. These are not the *only* expressions in mime, of course, but practice in creating these five expressions will increase the flexibility of your facial muscles, refine your control over those muscles, and expand your range of facial expression. These expressions are shown and described in Illustrations 1 through 5. In each of these expressions, your eyes will tell most of the story, but the rest of your face should naturally be consistent with what your eyes are doing. These facial expressions can be purely technical exercises, performed without emotion, or they can be used in an emotional context.

At first, practice these expressions in front of a mirror to see what you look like. After a while, practice without the mirror, and rely on your own inner awareness. It's very important in mime to learn to know how something *looks* by how it *feels*. Once you are familiar with the five basic expressions, and your face is no longer confused about which is which, try the exercises described below. The objectives of these exercises include concentration, total physical expression and control, and character interaction.

Exercises

INSTANT FACES (SOLO EXERCISE)

Have a leader, teacher, or friend call out the expressions, one at a time. Do each expression quickly—as *big* as you can and as *fast* as you can—then drop it immediately. It should take less time to *do* the face than it takes to *say* it. The leader should allow five seconds or so between expressions at first, then gradually decrease the time.

MELTING FACES (SOLO EXERCISE)

For this exercise, start with one expression—happiness, for instance. Decide on the next expression (or have a leader call it out), then slowly "melt" your face into that expression on a slow five-count. Hold the new expression for a few seconds, then move on to the next one. Make sure your face "melts" as a complete unit. As you practice this exercise, slow down the "melting" time.

A slightly more difficult variation is to start with one expression, then as *slowly* as you can, first melt from that expression to a *neutral* face, then melt to the next expression, again as *slowly* as you can: happiness, neutral, sadness, neutral . . . and so on. This exercise is very good for developing control of the facial muscles, and it's also good for developing concentration. The whole series of five expressions should take two or three minutes to complete at first, then even *longer* as you develop more control.

FACE AND BODY (SOLO EXERCISE)

The leader calls out one expression at a time. Assume a *total* body expression, body *and* face, that reflects that particular expression. If the expression is happiness, for instance, your face *and* body should express "happiness." Once you assume the expression, hold it without moving until the expression is changed. Each time you repeat an expression, try to vary the body. Explore as many physical variations of each expression as possible.

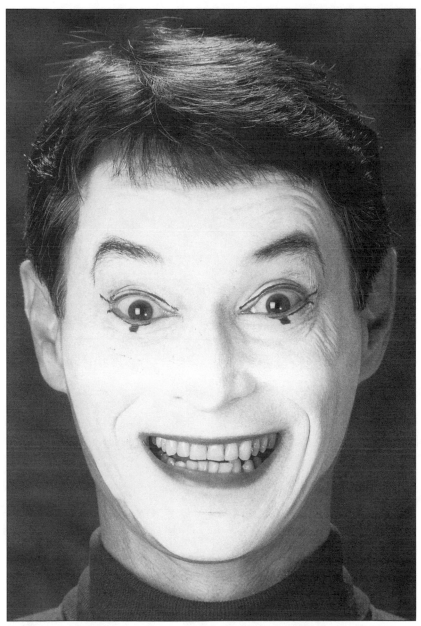

Illustration 1. Happiness. Lift your eyebrows. Open your eyes wide. Lift the muscles over your cheekbones. Make a big, happy smile.

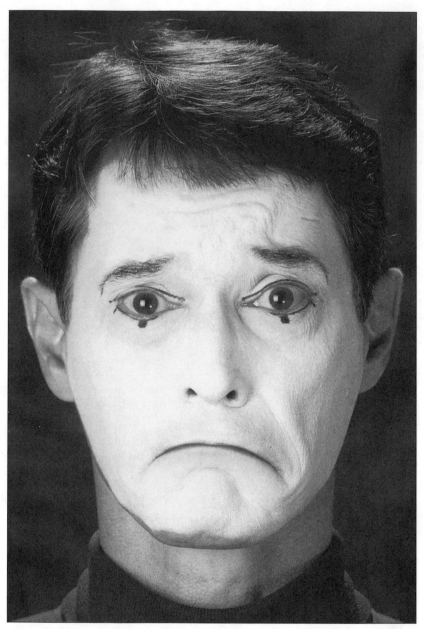

Illustration 2. Sadness. Bring your eyebrows together a little. Relax the muscles in your face. Frown. (Some people find it difficult to frown. Practice. A mime really ought to be able to frown.)

Illustration 3. Surprise. Lift your eyebrows. Open your eyes wide. Open your mouth as if to say "Oh!"

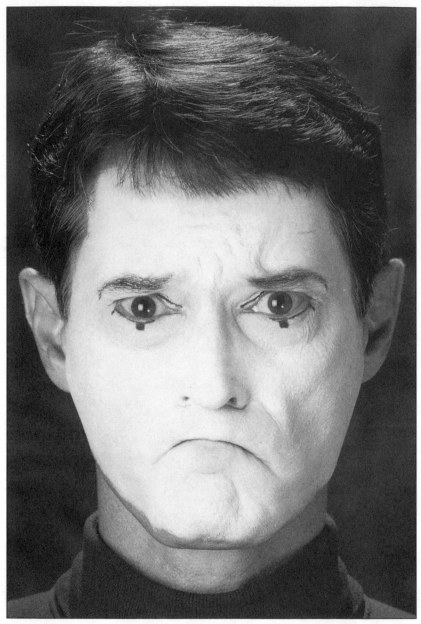

Illustration 4. Anger. Think of bringing all the muscles in your face in toward your nose. Furrow your eyebrows. Bring your mouth up in a tight-lipped frown.

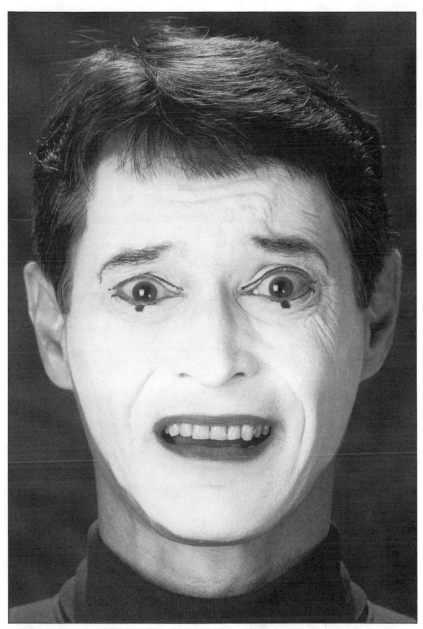

Illustration 5. Fear. In essence, "fear" is the upper half of "sadness" and the lower half of "happiness." Bring your eyebrows together slightly. Open your eyes a little wider than normal. Make a slightly strained "happy" smile—pull the corners of your mouth back as if to smile, and smile slightly, but not happily; just show some teeth.

SPLIT FOCUS (SOLO EXERCISE)

This is a variation of Face and Body in which the leader calls out *two* expressions. The first expression will be for the *face*; the second will be for the *body*. In other words, your face and body will be doing two *different* expressions at the same time. At first it will be easiest to do either the face or body, then *add* the other part. As you repeat the exercise, however, try to assume both the facial expression and bodily expression at the same time. Finish the exercise with a review of the basic expressions, body and face working *together,* as in Face and Body.

Split Focus is a challenging exercise. You will find it difficult at first, but with practice you should be able to assume any combination of expressions. As you become more proficient at this exercise, you also greatly expand your potential for physical expression.

EXPRESSION MILL (GROUP EXERCISE)

Begin by having a small group of students walk slowly around the room, in a random pattern, all staying fairly close together. The leader then calls out an expression. All members of the group must assume a total physical expression, face *and* body, and also *walk* in a style that reflects the expression. Walk "happy" or "sad," for example, while maintaining that particular physical attitude and facial expression.

Continue to walk in that manner until the expression is changed, at which time you should change instantly to the new expression—change your face, body, *and* walk at the same time. The leader should vary the time allotted to each expression, calling out expressions slowly at first, then gradually faster as the group becomes more proficient in the exercise.

INTERACTION (GROUP EXERCISE)

This exercise is based on Expression Mill and can flow directly out of that exercise.

Part One ■ Instead of changing expressions on command of a leader, do so each time you pass another person in the group. It's best to start this variation by walking slowly, to allow sufficient time to adjust to the changes of expression. Concentrate on changing expressions smoothly and evenly—face, body, *and* walk. Keep moving. There is a tendency in this exercise for the walk to deteriorate, even though the face and body may be doing fine. *All* the parts of your body must work together.

Part Two ■ Each time you pass another person in the group, *exchange* expressions. This will require a good deal of concentration from all involved. Make sure you give the other person enough time to figure out what *your* expression is before changing to *hers.* If you have no idea what expression the other person is doing, try to duplicate the expression as best you can, or simply move on to the next person. Be sure to keep your head up, and maintain eye contact. Keep moving, and concentrate.

Two-Person Interaction

Two people face each other from opposite sides of the room. They walk toward each other, with no expression, passing each other in the center of the area. They continue past each other for a few steps, still without expression. Both stop walking, and turn toward the audience. Each makes an expression (any expression), face alone or face and body together, and holds the expression for a few seconds. Both turn and exit, with or without expression. This is an interesting exercise to do and watch, and can be quite amusing.

Performance Piece

First of all, a few words about performance pieces. In mime, the ideal situation is solo performance. As a solo performer you have the undivided attention of the audience. You are able to express yourself freely, without any distractions or competition for the audience's attention from other performers.

In group pieces, the attention of the audience is considerably more widespread. There is simply more for the audience to look at. This should be taken into consideration when performing group pieces. All the members of the group should work together in a unified performance, not simply as individuals who happen to be together on the same stage at the same time.

Each member of the group must maintain a very high level of awareness and concentration. Everyone must work together and concentrate at all times.

Silent Movie

Each student/performer enters the performance area as if going into a movie theatre. Each performer defines his own character, her own role in the piece. Some may choose to be moviegoers, for instance. Others may sell concessions, be ushers, and so on. (Alternatively, the roles may simply be assigned by a director or leader.)

Scenario ■ The *Theatre Manager* enters first, unlocks the front door of the theatre, turns on the lights, and opens the ticket office. He is followed shortly by the *Ushers,* the *Ticket Seller,* and the *Concessions Person,* who arrives a little late perhaps. The *Ushers* prepare the theatre, check their flashlights, pick up odd bits of paper and ticket stubs. After apologies to the *Manager* for being late, the *Concessions Person* starts making popcorn and otherwise tries to look busy at the concessions stand. The *Ticket Seller* prepares to sell tickets, and the *Manager* walks around supervising.

Soon the *Moviegoers* start to arrive—singly, in pairs, or in small groups. They buy their tickets from the *Ticket Seller,* perhaps buy some popcorn or candy at the concessions stand, give the *Ushers* their tickets, and are shown to their seats. (If there are not enough *Ushers* to go around, the *Moviegoers* can find their own seats.)

The *Moviegoers* should form straight rows across the stage, facing the real audience. (Depending on the size of the group, two or more short rows may be preferable to one long one.) It is not essential or important for the *Moviegoers* to "sit" in their seats. In fact, it is much less awkward simply to stand in clearly defined rows. You can give the indication of a row of seats by how the *Moviegoers* move into the space and relate to one another.

When the *Moviegoers* have assembled in their seats, the lights go down . . . perhaps with one late arrival moving down the entire row to a seat, disturbing everyone in his path. The *Ushers, Concessions Person, Ticket Seller,* and *Theatre Manager* may join the group, forming their own row behind the *Moviegoers* or at the back of the movie theatre.

As the movie begins, all applaud . . . silently, of course. (One person could be designated as the "key" person to begin the applause.) All the *Moviegoers* (and the staff, if they're watching the movie) react to the movie, one expression at a time, in a predetermined order. The expression should flow smoothly from one to another—happiness, sadness, surprise, and so on, ending with happiness. This part of the piece is much like the Melting Faces exercise in the way that the group progresses from one expression to another.

At the end of the movie—a happy ending, of course—all applaud . . . again, silently. The *Moviegoers* leave the theatre in an orderly fashion, one or two perhaps lingering behind, watching the credits until the very end. When all the *Moviegoers* have gone, the

Concessions Person closes up shop, the *Ticket Seller* counts the money and closes up the ticket office, and the *Ushers* do a quick cleanup of the theatre. The theatre staff then leave the theatre, as the *Manager* holds the door open for them. The *Manager* turns off the lights, closes and locks the doors, and walks off down the street.

Performance Notes ■ One of the challenges of this piece is coordinating the changing expressions. All the moviegoers must be watching the same movie. It is essential that the expressions change *together.* This may sound almost impossible, but it really isn't too difficult. The moviegoers can look at one another, relate to one another, and "key" off one another, and thus coordinate the change of expressions. At first, it may be helpful to assign a certain number of counts, or "beats," per expression. In time, the moviegoers will sense when it is time to change expressions. Also, it may help for the moviegoers to use their whole bodies to change expressions, without exaggerating the body expression too much.

This exercise can be developed and refined in rehearsal to make an interesting and fun performance piece. The group will likely find many imaginative ways to interact during the movie. The overall aim of the rehearsals should be to center on exploring and developing the *total* environment of the moviegoing experience, rather than on any one particular aspect of it or on any one performer. (This is an ensemble piece, not a solo number with a backup group.) The moviegoers must stay aware, concentrate on the total environment, and not get caught up in an individual little "act" or ignore what everyone else is doing. The piece should last not much longer than five or six minutes, including all entrances and exits, and should progress smoothly, clearly, and efficiently.

Objectives for a group piece such as *Silent Movie* are concentration, development of ensemble awareness, coordination of activities, maintaining an environment, and character development within an ensemble performance. All of these objectives are vital to a good performance, and are particularly important to an effective group piece.

The Hands 3

One good thing about mime exercises in general and hand exercises in particular is that you can practice them anywhere, at any time, because you *always* have your equipment with you. Everything you need for mime travels with you wherever you go. The hand and finger exercises are challenging, but fun, and are important to your development as a mime. Use the odd moments of your day to practice your exercises—watching TV, waiting for the bus, or just walking down the street. Using those few "found" moments every day can help you greatly improve your mime technique.

When doing these hand exercises, keep your hands and arms as relaxed as possible. The overall objectives for the hand exercises are isolation and control of hand and finger muscles, coordination, concentration, space memory, and improvisation based on specific hand skills and techniques.

Warm-Up Exercises

HAND WARM-UP

Start with both your arms extended slightly in front of you, hands relaxed, palms down. First, *slowly* contract your fingers to make a tight fist with both hands. Next, slowly rotate your fists upward, then slowly extend and stretch your fingers up and out. Your palms should be facing forward at this point, and your fingers should be stretched out. Slowly close your fingers back in a fist as you rotate your hands down again. Finally, relax your hands and let your fingers hang down, palms down. Repeat the exercise.

Your hands should move slowly, but continuously, from relaxed . . . to fist . . . to stretch . . . back to fist . . . and then relaxed once again.

As a variation, begin with hands relaxed, palms down as in the basic warm-up exercise. This time, instead of moving both hands at the same time, begin with your right hand *only*. As your right hand starts to move from the fist to fingers extended, start the movement with your *left* hand. Continue the exercise in each hand, each hand moving on its own. Try to keep each hand moving slowly and smoothly, independent of the other.

FINGER WARM-UP

Begin with your hands in front of you, palms down, fingers straight. Rotate your first fingers only—clockwise, counterclockwise—then move them up and down and side to side. Repeat with your second fingers, and so on. Avoid moving other fingers, your wrists, or your forearms. Concentrate on isolating and controlling the individual fingers.

FINGER ROLL

Place your hands out in front of you, palms *up,* fingers straight. Starting with the little finger of both hands, slowly *roll* your fingers into your hands, one finger at a time, until your hands are closed. Open your hands in the opposite direction, from first fingers to little fingers. Alternate opening and closing your hands in this manner, by rolling your fingers into your hands. Try to develop a smooth and controlled rolling movement. As you increase your speed and proficiency, remember to keep your fingers moving smoothly, one at a time, with no breaks in the pattern. The visual effect should be of a "rolling" or "rippling" motion across your hands.

Some variations:

- Start from your *first* fingers instead of your little fingers. Close with your first fingers, open with your little fingers. Repeat.
- Close first fingers . . . *open* first fingers. Close little fingers . . . *open* little fingers.
- Start with the *first* finger of your right hand, and the *little* finger of

your left hand. Open in reverse. Although you'll be starting with different fingers in each hand, your fingers will be opening and closing in the same direction.

Put your hands in front of you, palms up, fingers straight, little fingers slightly touching, side by side. Starting with the first finger of your right hand, roll your fingers closed, in order, across *both* hands. Open in reverse, left to right. Open and close slowly and smoothly, one finger at a time.

Some variations:

- Roll your hands closed from the right, open from the left. (This will create a rolling motion.)
- Close left, open right. (Rolling motion.)
- Close right, open right. (This will create a ripple or wave effect.)
- Close left, open left. (Ripple or wave effect.)
- One hand palm up, the other palm down. Do the ripple or roll with your hands like this. Switch hands. Repeat the exercises.

First person starts the finger roll and ripple exercises. Another person comes along and watches the first person do the hand exercises for a short time. This second person moves next to the first person and puts her *open* hands up next to the first person's hands. As the finger roll motion travels down the first person's hands, the second person "steals" the motion and walks away with it, leaving the first person standing there empty-handed.

The first person then moves next to the second person and "steals" the motion back. The situation can be resolved by the two choosing to work together, or by one or the other running off with the motion.

As a variation, the two people can transfer the motion from one to the other by whatever means they can devise. They can hide it from each other, put it in a pocket, or even "toss" the motion back and forth like a ball.

Performance Piece

The hand piece and its variations can be put together into an interesting and challenging performance piece for a small group of up to eight people. It is essential that all the members of the group work together and remain aware of every other member of the group, in order to keep the piece moving smoothly and efficiently.

HAND PIECE

One person enters, doing hand exercises. Another enters, watches the first person for a short time, then "adds on" to the exercises. This continues, one new person at a time. Each new person "adds on" to the existing line of hands, until all in the group are in a line, with the hand exercises traveling down one direction, and returning the other direction.

"Rolling" hand exercises work best for this. As the second person moves to join in, the first person rolls his hands closed in the second person's direction. The second person takes up the exercise from there, and reopens her hands back in the direction of the first person. And so on. The variations are endless. Some possibilities:

The Wave ■ First person in line lifts his hands while closing the roll. Next person does the same, and so on down the line. The motion returns down the hands in the same manner. The height of the "wave" increases or decreases according to what the first person in line does with the exercise. The visual effect is of a rolling wave, increasing and decreasing in size.

End Around ■ First person in line starts the rolling exercise. As soon as her hands are closed, she quickly runs around the back of the group and joins up at the far end, opening her hands on the way. When that first person reaches the end of the line, she picks up the exercise as it comes down the line.

In the meantime, each successive person in line does the same thing—doing an "end around" and rejoining the group at the far end, until the line has reformed as it began. This can be repeated as many times as space permits. It is important that each person move quickly around to the far end of the group. The exercise moves quickly down the line, and each person has to be there and be ready to "add on." Also, everyone must remember to open their hands on the way around the back of the group.

Circle Roll ■ The group forms a circle, hands extended, palms up. One person begins a hand exercise, others follow in a clockwise or counterclockwise manner. Both "rolls" and "ripples" can be used for this exercise. If done for an audience, the circle of hands must be tilted toward the audience so the effect can be seen.

Exercises

THE WALL (SOLO EXERCISE)

This is a classic mime illusion. The exercise is particularly interesting because it illustrates very clearly the fine line between reality and imagination in mime. The audience "sees" something that is not there—in this case, an imaginary wall. If the wall is well defined by the mime performer, the audience believes they could somehow touch it if they were only closer. This is one of the joys of mime—the purposeful flights of imaginative fancy that the performer and audience are able to share.

Begin by imagining a wall about twelve to eighteen inches in front of you. Raise your right hand, and put *just the fingertips* of your hand on the imaginary wall. Your fingers should be fairly close together, in a natural way. Slowly press your hand against the wall, letting your fingertips move apart, until your hand is flat against the wall, with your fingers spread.

To take your hand *off* the wall, simply reverse the procedure . . . relax your hand back until just your fingertips are on the wall, then move your hand away from the wall.

Try the exercise with your left hand, repeating the movement as above, then right hand again, and finally with both hands (see Illustration 6).

The reason your fingertips are put on the wall first, and then your palm pressed against it, is to help more clearly define the wall for you and for the audience. The wall should not be too close to your body, or too far away. You should be able to press your hands against the wall without straining your wrists and forearms into unnatural or strained positions.

Start to explore your wall. Take your time. Move smoothly and deliberately. Put one hand on the wall, then the other, then take them off. Repeat. Put one hand on the wall, then the other. Take one hand off the wall, leaving the other where it is, and replace it a few inches up or down, right or left of its original position. Take your other hand off the wall and put it back, close to the first hand. Repeat with either hand. As you move your hands on the wall, try to "see" the wall for yourself, and try to "feel" it. You need to believe in the wall, in your imagination. If *you* do, so will your audience.

To move along your wall, first define the wall without moving. Then, depending on which way you want to travel on the wall, move both hands, *one at a time,* in that direction. First move the hand closest to the direction you want to go, then move the other. Hold your hands

Illustration 6. The wall. The hands are flat, with the fingers slightly spread.

motionless in space as you take a sideways step or two in the same direction that your hands moved. This will take a little practice. It's natural for your hands to want to move the same direction that you're walking. Concentrate on keeping your hands *motionless* where you put them. If your *hands* slide along the wall, it will look to the audience like the *wall* is sliding, too. Keep moving along the wall, to the right or left, then return to your starting point, then go the other way.

Sooner or later you will reach a *corner*. Let's assume you are moving along a wall to your right. To indicate an *inside* corner, first leave your right hand where it is on the wall. Next, take your left hand away from the wall. Cross your left forearm *over* your right forearm, and put your left hand on the second wall, your left hand at a right angle to your right hand (see Illustration 7). Drop your right hand from the first wall, and turn your body to face the second wall. Put your right hand on the second wall. You should now be facing the second wall squarely, both hands on the new wall.

If you are moving to the left, leave your left hand, which is closest to the corner, on the wall. Cross your *right* forearm over your *left* and continue the movement as above.

Continue moving along the wall, reaching corners as you go. No matter which direction you are going, when you indicate an *inside* corner, *always* leave the hand closest to the corner on the wall as you make the corner with the other hand. This will provide a frame of reference for the audience. If you take both hands off the wall, the audience will be confused about the illusion. If you're moving along a wall and drop both hands as you change direction, the audience will not know if your corner is square, round, or even there at all. Define for the audience *exactly* what you want them to see.

Outside corners are somewhat the opposite of *inside* corners. If you are moving to the right, leave your *left* hand—the hand *farthest* from the corner—in place. Move your right hand around the corner, to the new wall. Holding your right hand motionless in space, lift your left hand as you take a step or two around the corner, and replace your left hand on the new wall. Your arms will not cross. Your left hand will simply come around and take its position on the new wall.

To repeat: When doing an *inside* corner, leave the hand *closest* to the corner on the wall, and cross the other hand *over* it. For *outside* corners, leave the hand *farthest* from the corner on the wall, and proceed accordingly, without crossing your arms. Here are some tips for walls and corners:

- Keep your hands straight up, and your palms flat against the wall. Be aware of your thumbs. Don't let them stick into the wall. Put your thumbs in line with the rest of your hands.

Illustration 7. An inside corner. The left forearm is crossed over the right fore-arm, and the hands are at right angles.

- Be sure that both of your hands move on the same wall, which is to say that both hands move in the same flat plane.
- On the front wall, facing the audience, keep your hands at eye level and slightly apart so your face remains visible.
- On side walls (perpendicular to the audience), keep your hands close together, and occasionally touch your thumbs together to ensure that your hands stay in the same plane.
- On the back wall, move your hands up and out, well away from your body. Avoid obscuring the audience's view of your hands.
- When you move up or down a wall, be sure that you don't bend back and forth, into and away from the wall. Move your body with your hands as much as possible to avoid bending your wrists too much.
- If the wall is supposed to be solid, focus on the backs of your hands, and on the space directly between your hands.
- If the wall is transparent, look between your hands and focus on something in the distance.

THE BOX (SOLO EXERCISE)

Begin by deciding for yourself the dimensions of your box, with you on the inside.

First, define the front wall, the wall facing the audience. Explore this wall. Move a little left or right, up or down. Moving left or right, define the walls of the box all the way around, delineating the inside corners as your go. Keep the dimensions of the box constant.

When you come back to the front wall, you're on your own. Explore the possibilities—change the shape, let it close in on you, put a top on it, and so on. It's your box. Do what you like with it.

Side Walls ■ It is important that all the walls, particularly the side walls, appear flat and straight to the audience. Since the audience is looking directly down the side walls, they will notice the slightest variation in the plane of the wall. When you do a side wall, use the touch-the-thumbs technique. First, put your right hand on the wall. Then bring your left hand close to your right hand so that your thumbs are touching or nearly touching. This will help keep your hands on the same wall, in the same plane, as you move along the wall.

Front Wall ■ Keep your hands apart so that your face is visible to the audience. It's important that the audience be able to see your face so they know what you're thinking and where your focus is. The *audience* will look where *you* look. They want to "see" what you're looking at. You will also be able to look at your hands as you move them to be sure they're on the same wall.

Back Wall ■ Keep your hands *well* apart, up and away from your body. If your body covers your hands, the audience will not be able to see what you're doing. If your hands are up and out, it will also heighten the illusion for the audience. (You will not be able to control your hands as well as on the front or side walls, but the audience's perception is not as keen for the back wall as it is for the others.)

General Tips ■ If you want your walls to appear solid to the audience, focus your eyes on the backs of your hands or on the space *between* them. If you want your walls to be transparent, look *through* the space between your hands, and focus on something in the distance. Overall, take your time. Define the walls clearly. Keep all of your walls straight and flat, and your corners square.

LABYRINTH (GROUP EXERCISE)

This works best with a small group. One person, using the "walls" and "corners" techniques, begins to define a maze or labyrinth. In turn, others follow the leader through the maze, being careful to put all *their* walls and corners exactly where the *leader* put them.

Explore the possibilities of the maze. Change leaders each time you start a new maze.

Keep a clear image of the maze in your mind as you go through it. Concentrate. Be aware.

The true test of proficiency in this exercise is to *return* through the maze *exactly* the same way—same walls, same corners.

Imaginary Objects 4

*A*s with all other aspects of mime training and performance, defining imaginary objects is as much a mental process as it is a physical one. The process begins in the mind, in the imagination, and is then projected physically to the audience. You must know and understand the mental process to be able to sustain the physical expression of it.

Every object is a story in itself. It has a beginning, a middle, and an end, and all these elements must be clearly defined. The audience must know where the object comes from (not just "out of thin air"), what the function of the object is or how you are using it, and when you stop using the object. If any one of these things is unclear or missing from the performance, the audience will not "see" the object and will not comprehend or understand what you are doing.

The main objective in defining an object in mime is to isolate the single most identifiable characteristic of that object, its *essence,* and to communicate that characteristic to the audience. What is it about each object that "says" exactly what it is? A broom is just a stick until you *use* it. A door is just part of a wall until you *open* it. An apple is just a round "something" until you *polish* and *eat* it. And so it goes with every object. There is something clearly identifiable about every object that will cause the audience to "see" that object immediately. It's the mime performer's responsibility to determine just what that special something is.

Sometimes the most difficult objects to define clearly in mime are the most *common* objects, the ones we come in contact with every day. Clothes, doors, tables, chairs, are often a challenge simply because we take them for granted, and we also take for granted that the audience will understand what these objects are without much guidance. This is not the case, however. Each and every object must be clearly defined, no matter how "common" that object may seem to you or how easy to comprehend you may think it is for an audience.

You cannot, for instance, simply push open a door and walk through it, as you do in daily life. The audience has no frame of reference for what you are doing, and will probably be confused by your movements. Your movements may make perfect sense to you, but your audience will most likely not understand what you're doing.

Another point to remember regarding objects in mime is that even though the object is imaginary, it must still conform to natural, physical laws—the laws of gravity and motion, for instance. This is a simple concept, but one that is often overlooked in mime training and performance. The audience relies on what their basic instincts tell them and on what they have learned from their own practical experience—heavier than air falls, and lighter than air floats. In the *real* world, as the audience understands it, an object left in midair will fall to the ground. It will not simply float in the air unattended until you return to it. A door stays open until you close it. An object remains where you put it until you move it, on purpose, either by *watching* it move or by physically *moving* it.

One final important principle of imaginary objects . . . an object does not begin to exist when you first *touch* it but when you first *see* it. When you look at the object, the audience will only know that you are looking at "something," of course, not what the object is, but at least you will have their attention. From that point you can define the object physically, keeping in mind everything you need to communicate to them so they can see the object as clearly as you would like them to see it.

Questions to ask yourself about defining *any* object in mime:

- Where is it? Where is it when you first see it?
- What is this object's essence? What is its most distinguishable characteristic?
- How can you best define this essence?
- Where does this object come from? Where is it located in the imaginary environment?
- What is the object's function? What does it do, if anything? How is it used?

- What is the object's shape, size, weight? What other physical properties does the audience need to know or understand about this object?
- If you let go of the object, what happens?
- What do you do with the object when you're finished with it?

The following exercises will help you learn to define objects clearly, quickly, and efficiently. Try to keep in mind the points about imaginary objects that have been mentioned above, and keep the "object questions" in mind as you practice the exercises. There are many things to consider in creating imaginary objects, and these will start to come more naturally with practice.

Exercises

OBJECTS (SOLO EXERCISE)

This is really quite a simple exercise that you can do anytime, anywhere. After a while, you will find yourself doing it subconsciously. It will become part of your everyday activities, even when you're not actually thinking about doing it.

For this exercise, simply take any real object—a drinking glass, for instance—and *hold* it, *touch* it, *feel* it, feel the *weight* of it, the *shape* and *dimensions* of it, use it, and try to remember *everything* you can about it, particularly the movements you used in exploring it. Pick the glass up and put it down. Move it from hand to hand. Determine for yourself the *essence* of a drinking glass. What is it about a drinking glass that distinguishes it from any other object, and what distinguishes *this* drinking glass from every other kind of drinking glass that you can think of?

Now put the drinking glass down. Create the drinking glass in mime. Try to duplicate your earlier movements as precisely as you can. If you forget, pick up the real glass, refresh your memory, and try again.

Try this exercise with every object with which you come in contact. Explore every object you can, and file the object away in your "mime memory."

A DAY IN THE LIFE (SOLO EXERCISE)

This is a day in *your* life. Begin your day asleep. At the sound of your (silent) alarm clock, wake up, yawn, and turn off the alarm. Get up out of bed, and go through your usual morning activities as if you were preparing for another day at school or work. Do *everything* you usually do.

Once you are fully prepared to step out the door, realize that it's the weekend, that you don't have to be anywhere today, and go back to bed.

Some variations:

- Assume that you are late for work or school. Repeat your usual routine, but do it quickly, as if in a hurry. Again, once you are ready to go out the door, realize that it's the weekend. Breathe a sigh of relief, and go back to bed.
- Continue your morning activity through the whole day—condensed version, of course. Show getting to school or work, some work or school activity, lunch, afternoon activities, and so on, until you finally return to bed late at night.

PASS THE HAT (GROUP EXERCISE)

Actually, this could be Pass the Box, Pass the Basket, or whatever you like. A small group of six to eight students sits in a circle. One student (or the leader) defines a hat (or box or basket) in mime, and puts an imaginary object, clearly defined, into the hat. The hat is then passed to the next person in the circle, who also puts an imaginary object into the hat. This continues around the circle, each person putting something *into* the hat, until the hat returns to the first person.

When the hat reaches the first person, stop and discuss each object that was put into the hat. Was it clearly defined? What was the *essence* of the object? How could it have been defined differently or more clearly? Did the hat (or box or basket) remain constant in shape and size as it was first defined?

After the discussion, try the exercise again. This time, when the hat comes back to the first person, that person should take an object *out* of the hat, but it must be an object that the person didn't put in. The hat continues around the circle, each person taking something out, until the hat returns to the original person, empty.

Discuss the exercise again within the group. Ask the "object questions" again, not only about each object when it was put into the hat but when it was taken out. How consistent was each object? Was the object that was taken *out* consistent with the object that was put *in*?

SILVER TRAY (GROUP EXERCISE)

Instead of a hat (or box or basket), the leader defines a large serving tray. Each person around the circle then puts something on it—a plate, glass, silverware—that you might reasonably find on a serving tray. The point of this exercise is not only to define each object clearly, but to remember where each object was *placed* on the tray.

Again, once the tray has made it around the circle, send it around again, each person taking something *off* the tray until nothing remains but the tray.

SET THE TABLE (GROUP EXERCISE)

The leader defines a large table in the center of the room. Each person in the group will assist in setting the table for a formal dinner. Each member of the group is responsible for one type of object—plates, glassware, silverware, napkins. Don't forget the tablecloth, centerpiece, candles, and so on. Envision where each object would go on the table, and proceed accordingly.

You might take this exercise to its logical conclusion and all sit down to dinner. *Bon appétit!*

SUITCASE (GROUP EXERCISE)

This exercise is much like Pass the Hat, but there is an additional consideration—weight. Begin with a small group, about six or eight people, standing side by side in a line. The first person in line defines an imaginary suitcase and passes it, empty, down the line. The last person in line takes the suitcase back to the beginning of the line, opens it, and puts something into the suitcase. The suitcase is then passed to the next person in line, and then the next, each of whom puts something into the suitcase.

When the suitcase reaches the end of the line, that person carries it to the beginning of the line, and the exercise is repeated, until every person in line has moved to the beginning of the line.

At this point, the first person in line takes something *out* of the suitcase, and the exercise continues in like manner until the suitcase is empty.

This is a fairly long exercise and requires good concentration from all involved. You really have to pay attention to what goes in and comes out of the suitcase. Also be aware of the gradually increasing weight of the suitcase. By the time it is totally filled, it will be pretty heavy. Your movements should reflect the increasing and decreasing weight of the suitcase.

MOVING VAN (SOLO OR GROUP EXERCISE)

First, designate an area of the room that will serve as the moving van. Designate another area of the room as the house or apartment.

Imagine that the moving van is full of furniture and household effects—everything that you would ordinarily find in a household—and that the house or apartment is empty. Working singly, or in pairs, unload the moving van, and put all the furniture and household effects where they belong in the house. Coordinate your movements on "two-person" objects, such as sofas and refrigerators. Keep the objects consistent (and intact) while you move them.

You might designate a "sidewalk supervisor" to coordinate the unloading process and to decide where the furniture goes in each room in the house.

This exercise can also be performed in reverse—the house is full of furniture, and the van is empty. Load the van instead of emptying it.

Stay aware of the layout of the house, the doors, the walls, other furniture and appliances, and one another. Be careful to define each object, and to maintain the shape and weight of each object. (And don't *drop* anything. It could be an irreplaceable antique.)

Illusions 5

M ost of what occurs in mime is an illusion, of course—the imaginary objects, the imaginary costumes, the imaginary space. What I refer to here are the *illusions of motion*—the illusions of moving from one place to another, usually without actually going anywhere. For the most part, the illusions of motion are full-body activities, unlike the "smaller" illusions that involve only the hands, such as imaginary objects.

The illusions of motion described in this chapter (along with the utility illusions discussed in Chapter 6) are important mime exercises, as well as an essential part of a mime performance. They promote spatial awareness; bodily control, agility, and strength; and imagination. The movement necessary to create these illusions does not generally duplicate the movement as it is encountered in daily life, so you will have to practice diligently to make the illusions effective and believable. Illusions are indispensable for defining the movement of performers onstage, particularly when the *stage* space is actually smaller than the *imaginary* space needed for the performance. They are well worth the time and effort you will spend trying to master them.

In this chapter, you will learn the basic mime illusions that primarily involve the feet. In the next chapter, you will explore other mime illusions, as well as additional solo and group exercises and possible performance pieces. Following each illusion is a brief list of *dos* and *don'ts* to help you perform the illusion more effectively.

Walking

There are two basic types of illusory walking in mime: the *profile walk* and the *pressure walk.* Each illusion involves a different approach to mimed walking, and each is suited to a different type of performance situation.

PROFILE WALK

Begin by first warming up the muscles in your legs, particularly your ankles, which do most of the work in this illusion.

Legs and Feet ■ Standing up straight, transfer the weight of your body to your left leg. Lift your right foot from the floor to approximately midcalf level, letting your toes drop naturally toward the floor. (There is no need to point your toes.) Next, extend your right leg in front of you about the distance of a normal walking step and straighten your leg. As you do so, flex your right foot so the heel is pushed forward.

With your leg still straight, foot flexed, bring the right foot back to the floor, next to the left foot, in one smooth motion. It is acceptable to slide your heel on the floor, but be sure your toes don't contact the floor until the foot is all the way back where it started.

Repeat this part of the exercise several times with each foot.

Begin the leg motion again with your right foot. This time, as the right foot is moving back to the floor, flex the knee of your left leg so that your left heel is lifted from the floor. Think of lifting your heel rather than going up on your toe. This will keep your head from bobbing up and down while you perform the illusion. It is also much less tiring simply to lift your heel off the floor than to raise the entire weight of your body each time you go up on your toe.

Try the entire exercise up to this point several times with each foot. You may find it helpful to hold onto a chair at first, until you're better able to keep your balance.

Once you have a good idea of the overall leg and foot motion, begin to *alternate* the motion, as smoothly as possible, from foot to foot. Try to develop a normal walking rhythm. Be careful not to

Illustration 8. The profile walk. Arm and leg motions are parallel. The body is upright, perhaps even leaning slightly forward.

"travel" across the floor. The illusion is generally done in one place, without moving forward or backward. It is possible to move forward or backward for different effects, of course, but try to stay put while you're learning the exercise.

When your legs and feet are moving smoothly and you can hold your balance without assistance, you should add the arm motion.

Arms ■ Your arms should move in *opposition* to your legs, as they do in normal walking. When you actually walk, the movement of your body through space facilitates the arm motion. Your arms swing naturally. In mime, you have to do the arm movement on purpose, because there is no momentum or body movement to cause your arms to swing on their own.

The most effective method of learning the arm swing is simply to point to the bent knee with the opposite hand. In other words, as your left heel comes off the floor, your left knee will bend. Point to your left knee with your right hand at this point. This is where the swing happens. This will feel (and look) very artificial at first. In time, you will learn to coordinate your arm and leg motions so that they appear perfectly natural.

The arm and leg motions should be parallel. The body should be upright, perhaps even leaning slightly forward to indicate forward motion (see Illustration 8).

Getting the arm and leg motions just right is very difficult for some people. Others take to it right away. Even if it happens to be easy for you, make sure the timing is right and that it looks natural. What *feels* right may not always *look* right. Remember that awareness comes from knowing how something looks by how it feels.

Once you have the movement of the illusion under control, legs *and* arms, explore the illusion. Practice walking in an imaginary environment. Watch things go by as you walk—signs, traffic lights, cars and trucks, other people. Be sure that the object or person you are watching is moving by you at the same speed as you are walking. The illusion of walking rarely exists in a vacuum. What you *see* or *do* while you are walking in mime helps define the imaginary environment for your audience.

As its name implies, the profile walk is best viewed from the *side*. If you do turn toward the audience while performing this illusion, your arms should move slightly across the front of your body and your feet should turn out a little. Generally, it's best to start this illusion from the side, then turn toward the audience as you're walking.

PRESSURE WALK

Legs and Feet ■ Begin with both feet on the floor, about shoulder width apart, and with your weight slightly forward. Transfer your weight to your left foot, pick up your right foot, and put it down again, on the *ball* of the foot, in the same place it just came from. Transfer your weight to your right foot.

You will now slowly put your right heel back to the floor. As you do so, slowly slide your left foot *backward* a few inches, keeping in contact with the floor, and keeping your left leg relatively straight. Your left leg should stop moving backward at the same time that your right heel comes completely to the floor.

Bring your left foot forward, bending the leg a little, and put the ball of your left foot on the floor, as you did with the right foot. Repeat the motion as before—slide your right foot back as you bring the heel of your left foot to the floor. Repeat, alternating feet. Remember that your sliding foot should go straight back and should stop when the opposite heel reaches the floor. Work on developing a natural walking rhythm to the movement.

Arms ■ Your arms move in opposition to your feet, as in the profile walk. In the pressure walk, however, your arms will move slightly *across* your body rather than parallel to your foot movement (see Illustration 9).

Unlike the profile walk, the pressure walk can be performed from the front, side, or back with equal effectiveness. When performing the illusion from the front or back, let your sliding foot move out to the side and bring your arms across the front of your body a little more. From the side, slide your feet straight back and move your arms a little more parallel to your body.

USE IN PERFORMANCE

The profile walk and pressure walk serve different purposes in performance. The *pressure walk* is more practical in terms of getting from one illusion to another, and in moving from actual to illusory walking. Also, by varying the position that you replace your foot on the floor, you can actually move forward or backward and it will appear very natural to the audience.

The *profile walk* seems to have more of a character of its own and is more difficult to assume from actual walking; you will discover that it is less practical than the pressure walk in moving from illusion to illusion. You will need to experiment with each walking illusion to find the one most applicable to your performance situation.

Illustration 9. The pressure walk. Arms move slightly across the body rather than parallel to the foot movement.

DOS AND DON'TS

- *Do* focus outside yourself. Look off into the distance, and focus on your destination, for instance, or on other characters in your environment.
- *Don't* look at the floor (except within context of the piece). It reminds the audience that what you're doing is an illusion, and may inhibit their imagination, particularly if you remind them too often.
- *Do* remember to keep your head level while you walk. *Don't* bob up and down. In regular walking, your head stays relatively stationary in relation to the ground or the floor. Try to recreate this appearance in the illusion.
- *Do* let your walking reflect your emotional state. *Don't* let the illusion become mechanical, or purely technical. The illusion of walking (or any other illusion, for that matter) should be performed in context, as an integral part of the piece, not as a showy technical exercise added on for effect.
- *Do* keep in mind your physical relationship to the audience.
- *Don't* forget where you are in your imaginary environment. People subconsciously remember how many steps you took to get from place to place. Be consistent.

Exercises

The Crowd Scene and Bus Stop exercises help you build a sense of individual characterization within a group, develop group awareness, and show you how walking illusions can be used in a group setting.

CROWD SCENE (GROUP EXERCISE)

Part One ■ Form a small group, all facing toward the audience's right or left. Everyone begins the pressure walk at the same time, in a normal walking rhythm. Members of the group should relate to one another as they walk. After everyone has "settled in," each person in the group should try moving forward or backward, a little at a time, in relation to the others in the group. The group as a whole should not actually move forward or backward. The illusion is one of individuals in the group traveling at different speeds relative to one another and relating to one another as they walk.

Part Two ■ The group continues walking. The group then turns toward the audience, as a whole, as if walking around a corner. Everyone keeps relating to one another and continues walking and turning corners until the group returns to the starting position. Remember to keep together, stay aware of your relationship to the group, and relate to one another.

BUS STOP (GROUP EXERCISE)

One or two people begin an illusory walk facing toward the audience's right or left. (Either the profile walk or the pressure walk will work here.) If this is done by a small group, everyone should stay fairly close together.

The rest of the participants form a small crowd, off to the side, preferably out of view of the audience. This second group will face forward, and move *sideways,* in a heel-toe, heel-toe fashion, in the *opposite* direction from the one the first group is facing. (If the first group is facing right, for instance, the second group will move from right to left.) The second group will gradually move past the first group, upstage of them, at the same speed that the first group is walking.

The second group should relate to one another as if waiting at a bus stop—reading a newspaper, chatting amongst themselves, checking the time, and so on. The second group should keep their bodies fairly straight from the waist up, so only their legs and feet move.

This particular exercise is really three illusions at the same time: (1) the first group is doing an illusory walk, (2) the second group is moving sideways, and (3) it appears to the audience that the first group is walking past the second group when the *opposite* is true— the *second* group is actually moving past the *first.*

Try different combinations of illusions, and explore the possibilities of different individuals or small groups moving forward, backward, or sideways in relation to one another.

Going Up or Down Stairs

In giving the illusion of ascending or descending stairs, the motion of the feet and legs remains essentially the same, whether going *upstairs* or *downstairs.* The difference between the two is in the focus of the head and upper body and in the motion of the arms. The illusion is generally performed facing off right or left.

FEET AND LEGS

The pattern of motion is step-up-down. Start with both feet flat on the floor. Lift your right foot about eight inches off the floor and put it down on the ball of the foot, approximately six inches in front of where it started—step. Keep your right heel off the floor at this point.

Next, go up on the balls of both feet—up. Then, staying on the ball of the left foot, go down on the heel of the right foot—down.

Now, lift your *left* foot, and repeat the motion as for the right foot—step-up-down. Pick up your left foot and put it down on the ball of the foot, approximately six inches from where it started. Go up on the balls of both feet, and down on the heel of the left foot. Your right foot is now ready to go again.

Repeat the movements.

The important point here is to finish each step-up-down before you start again. The steps of the stairs should be distinct from one another, and should not overlap. Step-up-down, pause. Step-up-down, pause.

Be aware that you *will* move across the floor, about six inches at a time. This is not a problem. The space can be condensed, but for the illusion to be effective there should be some slight forward movement.

UPSTAIRS

Head ■ Raise your head slightly upward, and look in the direction that you would like the audience to think you are going up the stairs. Don't just raise your eyes. Actually raise your head slightly and look up the stairs.

Hand and Arm ■ Your hands and arms will define the stair railing, which will, in turn, help to define the stairs illusion as a whole (see Illustration 10).

First, extend your right arm, elbow slightly bent, straight ahead from your shoulder. Grasp the railing with your right hand. (The railing should be at a slight upward angle.) Your right hand and arm will move down the railing in *three* relatively equal sections: (1) on the first step, move your hand and arm, at a slightly *downward* angle, about halfway back to your body; (2) on the second step, continue to move your hand and arm to your side; (3) on the third step, move your hand and arm back and down past your body, with your arm straight. Release the railing, and repeat.

It will appear as if the *railing* is actually moving past *you* as you go up the stairs.

Now put the hand and arm motion together with the leg motion. Your arm and hand motion should be coordinated with your leg motion, so that your arm and hand move *only* when your legs are moving, as you go up on the balls of both foot. Avoid moving your

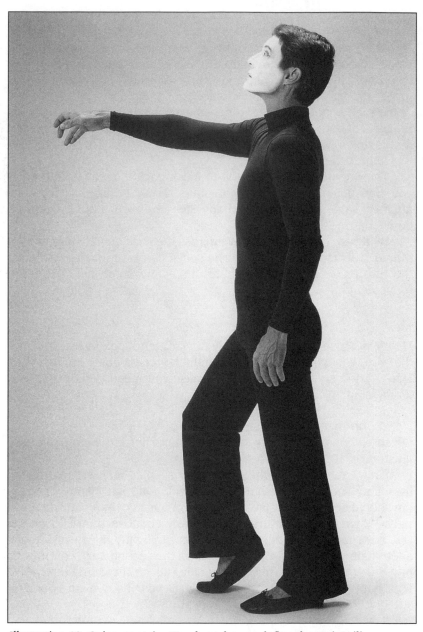

Illustration 10. Going up stairs. Hands and arms define the stair railing.

hand and arm up and down when your body moves up and down. Your railing should stay straight, and at a consistent angle.

Although this illusion is usually done from the side, and only one arm is used, your should be able to perform the illusion with either arm. In performance you will generally use the arm *farthest* from the audience.

DOWNSTAIRS

Head ■ Lower your head slightly, and look in the direction that you will be going down the stairs. Again, don't just lower your eyes. Actually lower your head a little.

Hand and Arm ■ Reach ahead and down, arm straight, and grasp the railing. Unlike in the upstairs illusion, your arm will move in only *two* sections: (1) on the first step, bend your elbow and move your hand halfway back to your body, on a slightly *upward* angle; (2) on the second step, move your hand, at the same angle, to your side. Let go of the railing, and repeat the motion. Again, move your arm and hand only when your legs move up onto the balls of both feet (see Illustration 11).

MOVEMENT SEQUENCE

The usual sequence of events in performing the stairs illusion are these:

1. Walk to the stairs.
2. Look up or down the stairs, depending on which direction you're going.
3. Grasp the railing.
4. Proceed up or down the stairs.
5. When you get to the top (or bottom) of the stairs, let go of the railing, and walk away from the stairs in a normal way.

By looking up or down and grasping the railing, you prepare the audience for the illusion, even before you actually begin the stair motion. Look, reach, go.

Overall, try to be very consistent with your hand and arm motion. Keep your railing straight. Be sure to let go of the railing after each series of two or three steps, and start by grasping the railing again for each series of steps. When your have a good grasp of the illusion, let your head move naturally as you go up or down the stairs. Rather than holding your head in a fixed position, think of

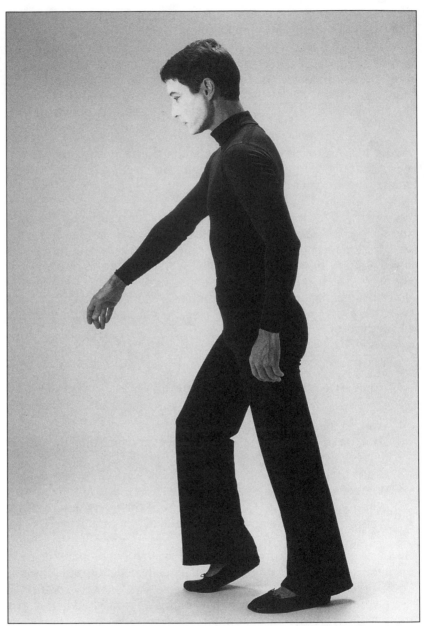

Illustration 11. Going down stairs. The arm and the hand move when you are on the balls of both feet.

watching the top step come down toward you, or the bottom step come up to you.

- *Do* focus. As with the walking illusions, it's important to actually look at something in the distance, like the top of the stairs, for instance.
- *Don't* space out, or go into your own private "stair illusion world." Stay in your imaginary environment, and help your audience stay with you.
- *Do* keep your railing straight. *Don't* bend, fold, or otherwise mutilate it. The audience's perception of the imaginary railing is very important to the overall effectiveness of the illusion.
- *Do* smooth out the step-up-down pattern for your feet. *Don't* stop or pause at the up. It may help to think of the movement in terms of step-up-over-and-down, or as a continuous motion rather than three separate movements.
- *Do* define the beginning and end of the stairs very clearly. *Don't* just walk into the illusion, or walk away at the end of the staircase. Take enough time to make the first and last steps you take just a little bit bigger, and give them a little more emphasis than the rest of the stairs.
- *Do* remember the sequence: look, reach, go. *Don't* try to take any shortcuts through the illusion, even if you are performing the illusion quickly—like running up or down the stairs, for example. Keep the audience with you every step (!) of the way.
- *Do* be consistent. *Don't* forget to count the number of stairs as you do them (you can be sure that someone in the audience will), and be sure that your stairs begin and end in the same place onstage.

In moving into and out of illusions such as walking or going up or down stairs, it may help to distract or *mis*direct the audience, as a magician would, to avoid drawing attention to the fact that you are doing an illusion. Make the audience look somewhere other than at your feet while you work your magic. You could, for instance, see something ahead of you on the street or at the top of the stairs that interests you, and look at it. The *audience* will look where *you* look, if only momentarily, and you can then slip easily into the illusion while they're distracted.

Exercise

MY HOUSE (SOLO EXERCISE)

Using the *stairs illusion,* the *walking illusions,* and *imaginary objects,* you will define your own house or apartment. Or you can define a totally imaginary one, if you like. (Later you can try this exercise again using the *doors illusion* from the next chapter. For now, do the doors as best you can.)

First, starting from outdoors, walk to your house. Enter. Walk through all the rooms. Stop in each room to define it somehow through imaginary objects in the room. Maintain a mental image of the layout of the rooms. Make sure you don't walk through the walls or trip over the furniture. Go up or down the stairs, as appropriate.

Retrace your steps, leaving your house the same way you came in.

There is an important concept in mime, the conservation of space, that you should keep in mind when you practice this exercise. Each time you repeat the exercise, try to condense the space, until you can define your entire house within a few square feet. This will seem very difficult at first, almost impossible, but by using the illusions that you've learned, you *can* do it.

Running

There are two basic techniques here, *real* running and *stylized* running.

REAL RUNNING

The first technique is simply running in place—*really* running but without actually going anywhere. You *do* have to slightly exaggerate the arm and leg motions for the illusion to work. Real running looks best to the audience from the side, of course, but you can do it at any angle to the audience, *and* you can easily move backward or forward while you run.

STYLIZED RUNNING

Because this illusion is stylized, and somewhat slower and less flexible than real running, stylized running is generally used in fantasy or dreamlike situations, particularly when you want to show the action of running in slow motion.

Illustration 12. Stationary running. When the near leg is bent, the far arm is in the forward position.

Stand facing toward the right or left. Bend slightly forward at the waist, and bring your arms up, elbows bent, as if you were going to start running. The leg closest to the audience will do most of the work. The leg farthest away from the audience will stay relatively stationary.

Lift the leg closest to the audience. Lift your knee high, then bring your leg back, straightening your leg as you do so and extending it behind you. Your foot should barely brush the floor in passing.

Bend the leg farthest away from the audience when the moving leg is extended toward the back.

Straighten the far leg when the knee of the moving leg is pulled forward.

You should pump your arms as if running, in a slightly circular motion, in opposition to the leg movement. When your *near* leg is bent, your *far* arm should be forward (see Illustration 12). When your *near* leg is straightened to the back (and your far leg bends) your *near* arm should be forward.

This illusion is best viewed from the side because of the limited motion of the legs.

It is possible to move from one type of running illusion to the other without too great a loss of illusory credibility. One such possible scenario would be to gradually move from real running, at normal speed, to stylized running in slow motion, and back again to real running.

DOS AND DON'TS

- *Do* expect to get tired. *Don't* shortchange the illusion to conserve energy. If you expect the audience to believe the illusion, you must run all out, all the time. It is harder to mime running than it is to run for real.

Exercises

THE CHASE (SOLO EXERCISE)

Begin by walking in place, using the pressure walk illusion. Walk easily, in a leisurely manner. Watch something or someone go by. While you're walking, periodically look back over your shoulder, as if you believe you are being followed.

Gradually increase your walking speed, still looking over your shoulder, until you are running in place—real running works best.

At this point, there are two alternatives. The first is to let yourself slowly slide backward while you are running *forward,* gradually losing ground, until you have moved completely out of sight, offstage.

The second alternative is to stay onstage but to gain and lose ground gradually while you are running. Continue running and looking over your shoulder, but gradually slow down as the danger seems to pass, until you are once again walking at a normal pace.

Try to progress smoothly from walking to running back to walking. Look over your shoulder occasionally to remind the audience that someone or something is following you.

WALKING AND RUNNING
(TWO-PERSON OR GROUP EXERCISE)

This exercise employs a triple illusion, somewhat like the Bus Stop exercise. There is the illusion of walking, of running, and of the slightly unreal relationship between the two. This exercise can be performed by two people or two small groups.

One person (or group) begins center stage, facing off right or left, walking—either the profile walk or the pressure walk. She looks at the audience and smiles, still walking. She continues walking through the following.

The second person (or group) enters from behind and slightly upstage of the first, running—real running works best for this. This second person continues running, gradually draws up next to the first person, and with considerable effort, finally passes her. Second person is very pleased with himself.

The *first* person keeps walking, watching the second person go by, perhaps tipping her hat or waving at the second person as he goes by.

When the running person has managed to pass the walking person by about six feet, he *slowly* begins to lose ground and gradually fall behind. The running person draws next to the walking person again, then slowly falls behind her. He runs harder and harder, but only succeeds in falling further behind, until he has moved completely out of view, offstage.

The walking person looks at the audience again, shrugs her shoulders, smiles again, and keeps walking.

The *walking* person should try to maintain the same walking pace throughout the exercise. The *running* person's speed will change, depending on how hard he is working—comfortably at first, then with considerably more effort as he falls behind.

The juxtaposition of these two illusions is very interesting to watch, particularly in terms of the effect of the piece has on the audience. The audience is caught trying to decide between reality and illusion, in a situation that is totally artificial and totally imaginary. Nevertheless, they "see" it in their imagination, and they try to reconcile what they see with reality, at least as they know it, or *think* they know it. The audience starts to doubt, if only for a minute, their own formerly unshakable concept of reality.

Skating

First of all, you need a smooth, clean floor, but one that is not too slippery. Be sure your legs and ankles are very well warmed up for this illusion.

Begin by standing on one foot, either foot, and move *to the side* by alternating heel-toe, heel-toe in a rapid manner across the floor. Go about three feet to the side, then repeat with the other foot. Keep your knees slightly bent. Relax, and let the motion flow cross the floor.

Next, try to develop a definite rhythm to your sliding motion—three repetitions of heel-toe in each direction. Pause on the last "toe" in each direction, push off from that foot, and slide into the movement in the other direction. Heel-toe-heel-toe-heel-toe, pause. Heel-toe-heel-toe-heel-toe, pause. One two three four five six, pause. One two three four five six, pause. Gradually increase your speed until you can move your feet as fast as you can say the words. Keep your knees slightly bent, and push off in the opposite direction, sliding onto the other foot.

Pick up your heel behind you as you slide to the opposite foot, but don't let the trailing leg cross behind the moving leg. Move the trailing leg up, back, and slightly out to the side rather than behind you.

Once you have the leg motion relatively under control, add the upper body movement, which should come fairly naturally. As you move to the right, for instance, *both* of your arms should lead in that direction, across your body to the right. As you slide to the left, lead with your arms to the left. Your arms should move up and away from your body to the side, in each direction. Your arms will help you keep your balance and will help define the illusion more clearly for the audience (see Illustration 13).

Even though your body is moving side to side, try to think of yourself as moving *forward,* as you would if you were really skating. Keep your head up and your eyes focused in the distance, on a point toward which you may be skating. The movement of the illusion may cover six feet or more from side to side, depending on your speed, the size of your heel-toe steps, the size of your feet, and your enthusiasm.

Illustration 13. Skating. As the body slides to the right, the arms lead to the right, moving up and away from the body.

By bending over at the waist and moving quickly from side to side, you will give the impression of skating quite fast. By standing more erect and assuming a more relaxed attitude and demeanor (with your hands clasped behind your back, for instance), you will appear to be skating at a much more leisurely pace. No matter your actual speed, your feet should move in the heel-toe motion fast enough to appear like you are *gliding* across the ice.

The skating illusion is most effective when viewed by the audience from the front or the back. The side view can be used effectively, however, when doing "figures," for instance, or in group skating situations. The illusion is not limited to ice-skating, of course. The illusion will serve equally well for roller-skating or in-line skating. As with any other illusion, you must prepare the audience for what they are about to "see." If you are ice-skating, you will need to set up an ice-skating environment—outdoors, cold, skating pond, and ice skates. Roller-skating and in-line skating can be done indoors or out, and you need to define the appropriate environment and the type of skates.

DOS AND DON'TS

- *Do* keep some part of the body moving at all times. *Don't* just glide along. The audience will not perceive that you are gliding without some part of you body in motion to sustain the illusion. Keep your arms moving out to the side, or do a slower, gliding heel-toe motion.
- *Do* devise some way to put your skates on and take them off. *Don't* just jump into the illusion. You may fall through the ice. (See the underwater illusion in Chapter 6.)
- *Do* think forward, ever forward. *Don't* think of the illusion as moving from side to side. Even if you're skating backward (a good trick, if you can do it), you're still going *forward,* only backward. (You understand.)
- *Do* remember to sustain the environment. *Don't* take for granted, for instance, that your audience will naturally assume that it's cold outside (if that's where you are). You must *show* them what you want them to know. Focus in the distance to give the audience a feeling of outdoors and of space.

Exercise

ILLUSIONS IMPROVISATION (SOLO EXERCISE)

Improvise with the illusions that you've learned so far. Decide to go skating, for example. Get your old skates out of the upstairs closet or trunk. Put on your coat, scarf, gloves, and hat, and walk to the skating pond or rink. Put on your skates. Slip-slide around for a while until you get the hang of it, then skate around. Challenge another skater to a race. Watch your fellow skaters skate off into the distance. Wave at them.

Explore different ways to define the skates and the skating environment, and different ways to use the illusions of *objects, walking, running, stairs,* and *skating* in improvised pieces.

Riding a Bicycle

This illusion requires strong and flexible ankles, good balance, a little coordination, and good stamina. Bicycle riding is not a particularly difficult illusion, but it can be very tiring, particularly when you are first trying to learn it. In fact, the hardest part of this illusion is just getting *on* and *off* the bicycle in a coordinated and *believable* manner.

FEET AND LEGS

The illusion is best performed facing off right or left. The foot farthest from the audience will remain relatively stationary. The foot closest to the audience will move in a circular pattern, as if pedaling a bicycle. Keep the circling foot parallel to the floor all the way around.

Each time the circling leg reaches the down stroke of the pedaling action, bend the knee of the stationary leg, going up on the ball of that foot (as in the profile walk). Continue raising and lowering the knee of the stationary leg to coincide with the movement of the pedaling foot. Smooth out the action. The illusion should look as if *both* feet are pedaling, even though only one foot is actually circling in the air.

The pedaling foot should not touch the floor. All the weight of your body is on your *stationary* leg, even though you have to move that leg as well. As in the profile walk, don't try to lift the entire weight of your body up and down when you go up on the ball of your foot. Simply bend your knee and let your heel come off the floor. It's much easier than lifting the entire weight of your body over and over again.

UPPER BODY

Bend slightly forward at the waist, and grasp the handlebars. Keep the handlebars even and stationary. They shouldn't wobble or move up and down. Turn the handlebars as you would on a real bicycle, of course, but otherwise try to keep them motionless in space. Think of riding a *real* bicycle—the handlebars generally stay in one place (see Illustration 14).

Illustration 14. Riding a bicycle. The body bends slightly forward at the waist, hands grasping the handlebars. The handlebars are kept even and stationary.

As previously mentioned, this illusion is best viewed from the side. For the illusion to be most effective, the pedaling motion should be fairly fast, but not a blur of speed. Once you have clearly defined the illusion, you can vary the speed of your pedaling to suit the performance situation.

DEFINING THE BICYCLE

Getting on and off the bicycle can be challenging. You can't simply stand in the center of the stage and start pedaling furiously; you first need to define the bicycle as you would define any other object. You also need to indicate to the audience where you and your bicycle have come from, and where you are going on your bicycle.

The following sequence of movements should help you define the bicycle for the audience:

1. Stand beside your bicycle, holding on to the handlebars with one hand and the seat with the other.
2. Raise the kickstand with your foot, and roll the bicycle forward.
3. As the bicycle is rolling, jump on; be sure to bring the handlebars in line with your body.
4. Once you're settled on the bike, and you have your balance, start pedaling.

Since it's difficult to show "putting on the brakes" in mime, when you have finished pedaling, simply jump off the bike as it slows down, run or walk beside it for a short distance, and come to a stop. Lower the kickstand (don't forget the kickstand), pat the seat, and walk away.

Getting into and out of this illusion is as important as the illusion itself. Set up the premise, define the bicycle, and then perform the illusion. The whole story has to go together in a logical manner that can be easily perceived by the audience.

DO'S AND DON'TS

- *Do* remember that the handlebars are solid, and stationary. *Don't* bend them all over the place while you try to maintain your balance. Remember, too, that the seat is *also* solid. If you happen to come down hard on the seat, for whatever reason, be sure to react accordingly.
- *Do* keep your foot motion going. *Don't* just coast. As long as the bicycle is in motion, you have to pedal. If you stop pedaling, the audience will think you have stopped moving. If that's what you

want them to think, no problem. If not, keep pumping those pedals.

- *Do* define the bicycle itself very clearly. *Don't* assume that the audience will understand what you are doing solely from the pedaling illusion. The definition of the bicycle is an integral part of the illusion.

Performance Piece

THE GREAT BICYCLE RACE

This can be performed by a group of up to ten or twelve. The characters in the piece include the crowd, the hero, the hero's girlfriend, the vendor, the mayor, and the villain.

Scenario ■ The performers who will form the *Crowd* enter—singly, in pairs, or in small groups—and gather in the center of the performance area. The general attitude and environment should be one of an important race—at a local fair, for instance. The mood should be festive.

The *Vendor* enters and joins the *Crowd,* selling popcorn and candy.

The *Hero* enters, in all his glory, accompanied by the *Hero's Girlfriend,* followed by their entourage, or a few well-wishers or hangers-on. The entourage joins the *Crowd,* as the *Hero* and his *Girlfriend* accept the accolades of the *Crowd. Hero* and *Girlfriend* embrace and kiss. *Girlfriend* throws kisses to the *Crowd.*

The *Villain* enters, in all his villainy, to the jeers of the *Crowd,* who throw popcorn and candy wrappers at him. He is not pleased, and behaves in his most villainous manner. He berates the *Crowd,* and leers villainously at the *Girlfriend,* who takes refuge behind the *Hero.* The *Hero* offers the *Villain* a handshake, which the *Villain* scorns, to the derision of the *Crowd.*

The *Mayor* enters, with appropriate pomp, waves to the *Crowd,* shakes a few hands, and beckons to the *Hero* and the *Villain* to get their bicycles for the race. The *Hero* and the *Villain* define their bicycles and roll them to the starting line, center stage.

The *Girlfriend* runs to the *Hero* for one last kiss. The *Crowd* cheers and the *Villain* sneers at them.

For the start of the race, the *Hero* is closest to the audience. The *Villain* is upstage of the *Hero,* and slightly ahead of him, trying to sneak ahead of the starting line. The *Mayor* takes his place ahead of the *Hero* and the *Villain,* and ushers the *Villain* back to the starting line.

The *Mayor* raises his starting pistol (or a scarf or his hand). As he does so, the *Crowd* becomes very still, in anticipation of the start of the race. All eyes are on the *Mayor* as he shoots the pistol (or drops the scarf or his arm). The race is on!

At this point, two things happen simultaneously. The *Hero* and the *Villain* both jump on their bicycles and start pedaling furiously. The *Mayor* moves back into the *Crowd,* which forms a circle, all facing out. The *Crowd* begins a heel-toe, heel-toe side-step motion, moving in a circle *opposite* the direction that the *Hero* and *Villain* are pedaling. The illusion is of the *Hero* and *Villain* racing on a circular track, with the *Crowd* in the background, urging them on.

The *Villain* attempts as many nasty tricks as he can think of in order to win the race—trying to knock the *Hero* off his bicycle, attempting to distract him, and so on. The *Hero* perseveres through it all.

Meanwhile, the *Crowd* continues to circle in the background, and react to the activities of the *Hero* and the *Villain.* There should be much pointing, waving of arms, jumping up and down, and other appropriate *Crowd* activity.

The race continues for a short time, with the *Hero* and the *Villain* exchanging the lead, the *Villain* behaving badly, and the *Hero* overcoming every obstacle. The *Hero* and *Villain* move back and forth in relation to each other, and upstage and down, by hopping on the stationary leg at an appropriate point in the pedaling motion.

To end the race, the *Hero* and *Villain* must have switched places—the *Villain* closest to the audience, the *Hero* upstage and slightly ahead of the *Villain.* The *Hero* draws himself up, and with one mighty, manly blow, knocks the *Villain* right off his bicycle. The *Crowd* reacts accordingly.

The *Villain* now executes continuous backward rolls, around the circling *Crowd,* as if left tumbling on the track as the *Hero* continues to the finish line. The *Villain* comes around again, still tumbling. The *Hero* runs over him with his bike, and just keeps pedaling.

As the *Crowd* comes around the final time, the *Mayor* steps out of the *Crowd* to indicate the finish of the race, by waving a flag perhaps. The *Hero* jumps off his bike just as the *Villain,* battered and broken, stops at his feet.

The *Girlfriend* runs to the Hero, showering him with kisses. The *Mayor* gives him a trophy. The *Crowd* goes crazy, congratulating the *Hero,* patting him on the back, shaking his hand, tossing popcorn, and so on.

The *Villain* tries to rise to his feet in the midst of all this, only to be pushed back to the ground by the *Crowd.*

Finally, the *Hero* takes the arm of his *Girlfriend,* and leads her and his adoring public offstage, all stepping over the vanquished *Villain* on their way. When all have left the stage, the *Villain* rises painfully to his feet, brushes himself off, shakes his fist at the heavens, and drags himself offstage, scowling over his shoulder and muttering villainous thoughts to himself.

Performance Notes ■ *The Great Bicycle Race* should be played for laughs, in a somewhat melodramatic style. The villain should be villainous, the hero should be heroic, the girlfriend should be beautiful and voluptuous, and the crowd should be boisterous and active. Members of the crowd must remember to stay close together, and to move as a unit in the circling motion. Their reactions while circling should be no less boisterous than when standing still.

This piece can be very effective if all involved work very closely together. The audience should have no trouble at all following the action if care is taken to ensure that the entire piece flows smoothly and clearly. Do not, however, sacrifice technique for a laugh. The humor of the piece comes from *within* the piece—the illusions, the stereotypical characters and their relationships—and should not be *imposed* on the piece.

The triple illusion of the crowd movement, the bicycle racers, and the relationship between the two will have the same visual effect on the audience as the Bus Stop, Crowd Scene, and Walking and Running exercises. *The Great Bicycle Race* is fun to do and fun to watch, and can be a very effective performance piece.

More Illusions 6

*T*his chapter deals with a number of "utility" illusions and exercises that you can explore and use in improvisations and performance. Some of these illusions, like *pulling a rope* or *walking a tightrope,* can stand alone, and others, like *going through doors* or *riding an elevator,* require a larger context in which to be most effective.

Pulling a Rope

The illusion of *pulling a rope,* like the illusion of riding a bicycle, is a combination of an object *and* a motion. You have to maintain the illusion of the *object*—the rope or the bicycle— *while* you perform the illusion of *motion* using the object. In other words, for this illusion you have to first define the rope before you can perform the illusion of *pulling* the rope.

THE BASIC ILLUSION

Stand facing front, feet shoulder width apart, knees slightly bent. Slide your upper body to the right, until your left leg is straight. Keep your head up, and bend your upper body to the right. Reach to the right with your *right* hand, about waist level, and grasp your rope. (You can use a rolling finger motion to wrap your hand around the rope to define it more clearly.) Reach across your body with your left hand, without turning your body to the right, and grasp the rope with your left hand, again at waist level. Your hands should now be between eighteen and twenty-four inches apart, grasping the rope.

Using your whole body, lean away from the rope. Slide your upper body to the left, straightening your *right* leg, and pull the rope along with your arms. Your hands must move together and remain the same distance apart as you pull (see Illustration 15).

When your upper body stops sliding to the left, stop the pulling motion of your arms and hands in front of your body with your right forearm against your right side.

From this position, lean your upper body to the right, and reach across your body and grasp the rope with your *left* hand, holding tight to the rope with your *right* hand at your side. Slide your upper body to the right again, as you reach with your *right* hand farther down the rope, past your *left* hand.

Repeat the pulling motion.

Remember to hold your pulling position all the way to the left when you stop pulling the rope. Reach across your body with your *left* hand first, then stretch out your right as you slide your body to the right. This maintains the illusion of tension on the rope. This illusion is very *isometric*—you use your own strength against yourself to help define the illusion. You need to use your whole body to define the tension on the rope, not just your hands and arms. (Think of an entire football team at the other end of the rope.)

Repeat the exercise a few times from this side, then practice pulling the rope from the other direction. Simply reverse the movements to the opposite side. Experiment with the illusion. Define different thicknesses of rope, the tension of the rope, the amount of strength needed to pull the rope, and so on.

The illusion of pulling a rope is best viewed from the front, with the rope being pulled from left to right or right to left across the stage. A diagonal line can be effective in some instances (as in Tug-of-War, described below).

DO'S AND DON'TS

- *Do* define the rope clearly. *Don't* assume the audience knows what you're pulling. Show them. Use your hand exercises to roll your fingers around the rope, for instance.
- *Do* keep the rope level, and at a constant distance form the floor. *Don't* confuse the audience by pulling on different ropes at dif-

Illustration 15. Pulling a rope. The upper body slides to the left as the right leg straightens. The rope is pulled along with the arms, hands moving together and remaining the same distance apart.

ferent levels. Use your body as a frame of reference to keep the rope and its distance from the floor consistent throughout the illusion.

- *Do* maintain a constant tension on the rope. Use your whole body, not just your hands and arms. *Don't* inadvertently let go of the rope during the course of the illusion. Release it only on purpose.

Exercise

TUG-OF-WAR (TWO-PERSON OR GROUP EXERCISE)

An individual (or a small group) enters the performance area and crosses to center stage. He notices a rope lying on the floor. He picks up the rope, looks offstage in the direction that the rope is going, pulls it tight, and begins the rope illusion.

Once the rope has been sufficiently defined for the audience, another person (or small group) enters from the opposite side of the stage at the other end of the rope, as if being pulled onstage by the first individual or group.

From here, it's basically an improvisation with the Tug-of-War illusion, each person or group taking and giving ground.

This exercise can be resolved in several ways: (1) someone walks onstage and cuts the rope and both people or groups fall down; (2) one person or group suddenly lets go of the rope, sending the other sprawling; (3) one person or group pulls the other completely offstage, out of sight.

It is essential that the people at each end of the rope work very closely together, coordinating their activities and remaining constantly aware of the activities of those at the *other* end of the rope. Both sides have to work to maintain a constant tension on the rope, to make sure that the give-and-take is well coordinated, and that each side reacts *realistically* and *believably.* Everyone should be on the same side of the rope, facing the audience, even though they will be pulling in opposite directions. The rope can be pulled directly *across* the stage or it can be pulled at a slight *angle* to the audience.

Going Through Doors

There are many different types and styles of doors, of course—doorknob doors, swinging doors, revolving doors, pushbar doors, and so on. Doors, like any other objects that we take for granted in our daily lives, require just as much practice and concentration as the more difficult illusions. Most of these different types of doors are not at all difficult to mime, once you are aware of the basic principles of the illusion. Perhaps the most complex door to mime effectively is the "doorknob door."

DOORKNOB DOOR

Begin this illusion by first approaching your door and stopping squarely in front of it. It will be helpful for you to use the floor as your frame of reference for your door. (Pick a mark on the floor for the position of the door when it's closed, so that you can return it to that very same mark after it's been opened.) Reach across your body with your right hand and grasp the doorknob, which should be positioned about waist-high, toward the left side of your body.

Turn the doorknob. (You'd be surprised how many people forget to do that.) Push the door slightly open. You could use your left hand to help push the door open, but be careful not to push your left hand *through* the door.

In order to avoid the door frame on your left, you will need to take a small sidestep to your right as you push the door open further. (Try this movement with a *real* door, and you'll soon discover the reason for the little sidestep.) Continue to push the door open with your right hand on the doorknob (see Illustration 16).

Take two steps forward, left foot first. Be sure that the door and doorknob come *with* you and that the door opens in a natural arc, pivoting on its hinges.

Take a small semicircular step to the right with your left foot. You should be turning to face the door. Put your left hand around the back of the door, onto the opposite doorknob. Release the doorknob in your right hand.

Move your feet to avoid running over them with the door, and close the door with your left hand on the doorknob, making sure the door pivots in a natural arc on its hinges and that it returns to its original position. Close the door with one small, final push. You should be facing the closed door, leaning slightly forward, with your left hand on the doorknob. Let go of the doorknob, turn, and walk away.

To return through the same door, simply reverse the order of movements. Remember that the door will open *toward* you on the return trip.

Experiment with the illusion to accommodate different types and sizes of doors and the direction in which each opens and closes.

Illustration 16. Going through a door. The door is pushed open with the left hand on the door and the right hand on the doorknob.

Doors are very familiar to an audience. One slight mistake or loss of concentration can ruin the whole illusion. See the door clearly in your own imagination, and concentrate on what you're doing to hold the illusion for the audience.

- *Do* remember that the doorknob is solid. *Don't* squeeze it or crush it.
- *Do* keep the door the same width throughout the illusion. *Don't* stretch the door as you walk through it, or condense it as you close it.
- *Do* keep the doorknob at a consistent height from the floor. *Don't* slide the doorknob up and down as you open and close the door, or move it back and forth. Use your body as a frame of reference for the doorknob.
- *Do* leave the doorknob on the door. *Don't* pull it off and take it with you when you walk away from the door. Let go of it.
- *Do* watch out for your feet. *Don't* run over them with the door. Get out of the way.
- *Do* be careful of the door frame. *Don't* run into it. Take a little sidestep to avoid it.
- *Do* close the door all the way to its *original* position. *Don't* forget where it came from. Use a mark or spot on the floor to guide you. (No, it's not cheating. It's being aware of your real environment, and using it to help you maintain your imaginary one.)
- *Do* practice. *Don't* take this illusion (or any other illusion) for granted.

Exercise

LABYRINTH II (GROUP EXERCISE)

This is based on the Labyrinth exercise in Chapter 3. In this variation, the first person through the labyrinth should add doors of all shapes and sizes to the walls and corners of the maze. At no time, however, should the leader cross through open space. Always maintain contact with one or more surfaces of the walls of the maze. The doors are positioned *in* the walls of the maze, not separate from them. Keep in contact with a wall on either side of the door. Let go of the wall only *after* you take hold of a doorknob, and define the wall inside the door *before* you let go of the doorknob on the other side of the door.

Climbing a Ladder

There are two ways to perform this illusion with your feet. The first way is slightly less challenging than the second, but both are equally effective in performance.

FEET FOR LADDER I

In this illusion, the feet move in much the same way as in the stairs illusion, but without moving across the floor.

First, standing up straight, facing right or left, pick up your right foot as if to step up on the rung of a ladder. Then put your right foot back down on the floor, on the ball of your foot. As you push the heel of the right foot to the floor, *simultaneously* rise up on the ball of your left foot. Pick up your left foot as if to step up on the next rung of the ladder, put it back down on the floor on the ball of the foot, and repeat the movement.

Remember to pause momentarily between steps, and to begin each new step by picking up each foot and putting it down on the ball of the foot as if placing it on the next rung of the ladder.

FEET FOR LADDER II

Pick up your right foot, placing it *flat* on an imaginary rung of the ladder, about a foot above the floor. As you push your right foot flat to the floor, rise up on the ball of your left foot. These two movements happen *simultaneously*—your right foot goes to the floor as your left foot rises to the ball of the foot. Pick up your left foot, and repeat the movement.

To keep your ladder straight, each time you pick up a foot to place it on the next rung of the ladder, pick it up slightly backward, in a semicircular motion, before you place it on the next rung. This way you can put your foot back down to its original position without moving forward, and it will give the illusion of bringing your foot up and over to the next rung.

ARMS AND HANDS

This sequence of movements for the arms and hands will work equally well for either type of leg motion.

Illustration 17. Climbing a ladder. The left hand grasps the lower rung at nose level, the right hand grasps the upper rung a foot higher, and the right foot steps on the rung.

Begin by grasping a rung of the ladder with your right hand, at the level of your nose. With your left hand, grasp a rung of the ladder about a foot above and slightly to the left of your right hand. (One hand should not be directly above or below the other.)

Before adding your feet to the hand movement, practice moving your hands straight down, at the same time, keeping a constant distance between them:

1. Your right hand is at the level of your nose, and your left hand is a foot above and slightly to the left of your right hand.
2. Slide both hands down together, maintaining an equal distance of about a foot between them. Your left hand should now be at the height of your nose, and your right hand a foot lower.
3. Take your right hand off the lower rung, and grasp a rung a foot higher and slightly to the right of the left hand.
4. Repeat the sliding motion, and continue alternating hands.

FEET AND HANDS TOGETHER

Basically, your hands should move down as the foot you have on the rung of the ladder moves down. When your foot stops moving, so should your hands. The sequence of events is this:

1. Grasp the lower rung with your left hand at nose level.
2. Grasp the upper rung with your right hand a foot higher.
3. Step on the rung with your right foot (see Illustration 17).
4. As your right foot (or right heel in Ladder I) moves to the floor, your hands should slide down—right hand to nose level, left hand a foot lower.

HAND AND ARM VARIATIONS

Instead of grasping *different* rungs with your hands, grasp the same rung with both hands, or the sides of the ladder. The same principle of sliding your hands as your foot goes to the floor still applies.

GETTING OFF THE LADDER AT THE TOP

First, decide which rung will be the top of the ladder as you go up. When this rung reaches your nose level, grasp it with both hands at the same time. On the next step, bring it down to chest level, then to your waist, and finally to your knees. From here you can step over the top of the ladder.

Be careful not to put your foot through the top rung. Hold onto the top rung with one hand until you step over it.

GOING DOWN THE LADDER

Reverse the sequence of movement in the arms and feet. Instead of lowering your arms and hands, for instance, you will raise them. Instead of pushing the rung down with your foot, you will lift your foot from the floor.

To come down from the top of the ladder, reverse the sequence noted above for getting off at the top. Climb over the top rung, and position both hands on the top rung at about knee level. As your move your feet, raise the top rung to your waist, then your chest, and finally to your nose. Proceed from there, down the ladder. You can continue down the ladder and simply step off and away from the bottom rung when your reach it, or you can jump off the ladder a few rungs from the bottom for a more dramatic finish.

DO'S AND DON'TS

- *Do* pause slightly between steps on the ladder. *Don't* rush. Take your time.
- *Do* stay in one place. *Don't* creep across the floor. The illusion is of going *up* only.
- *Do* make sure your hands and feet move precisely together. *Don't* confuse the audience by moving your hands and feet at different times, or by slightly overlapping the movements.
- *Do* keep your hands a consistent distance apart, on separate rungs, except when your hands are on the same rung. *Don't* expand or condense the space between the rungs. Remember that the ladder is solid. Use your body as a reference for the placement of your hands.

Exercise

WALKING A TIGHTROPE (SOLO EXERCISE)

This exercise can also serve as a solo performance piece in its own right.

Begin by using the climbing-a-ladder illusion you've just learned; climb up the ladder to the tightrope platform, high above the floor. When you reach the top of the ladder, step off onto the small platform. Steady yourself, and look far below to the floor beneath you, to your imaginary audience.

Extend your arms to your side to balance yourself. Pick up your right foot, and slowly *slide* it onto the wire. (Sliding your foot on the

Illustration 18. Walking a tightrope. Throwing the arms slightly off balance gives the illusion of trying to maintain balance.

wire helps to better define the illusion.) Step out onto the wire, and slide your left foot in front of your right, and continue to take small, careful steps across the wire to the platform at the opposite end. Slide your foot a little into each step.

While you walk across the tightrope, try to maintain a little bounce in your legs, a little up-and-down motion, that will convey to the audience the weight and movement of your body on the tightrope. This will also help the audience "see" the tightrope more clearly.

Keep your eyes up. Look at your feet only to take a step, if necessary. You don't want to remind the audience that you are actually standing comfortably on the floor.

To give the illusion of trying to keep your balance, actually throw yourself slightly off balance with your arms. This movement will appear to the audience as if your are trying to maintain your balance, which you *are,* but they'll think it's a result of walking the tightrope, not of you throwing yourself off balance on purpose (see Illustration 18).

If you should really lose your balance or start to fall, throw your arms up in the air, and go into a *slow motion* falling turn, until you land on the floor. (You can also use this effect on purpose.) It's best *not* to lose your balance, of course, but if you do, you now have a way to save the illusion.

After you have managed to cross the tightrope a few times without falling off, explore the illusion, and experiment with some variations—walk across with a balancing pole, blindfolded, or on a bicycle, perhaps.

Riding an Elevator

The basic technique of the elevator illusion involves setting the scene so the audience clearly understands what you are doing. The illusion itself is really quite simple.

Approach the elevator, facing *away* from the audience. Push the "Up" or "Down" button next to the door of the elevator. (Be sure to position the buttons far enough to the side of your body so the audience can see what you're doing.) Raise your head and watch the floor numbers above the elevator door, waiting for it to arrive at your floor.

When the elevator gets to your floor, drop your head, and watch the doors open. Walk into the elevator, and turn around to face the audience. Watch the doors close. Push the button inside the elevator for the floor you want.

Remember the laws of physics . . . as the elevator begins to move, up or down, you should react with your body *opposite* to the direction the elevator is traveling. If the elevator is going *up,* for example, you should sink a little in the knees when it starts moving, then straighten up slowly as the elevator continues to rise. When the elevator slows down and stops at the top, momentarily rise up slightly on your toes as it does so, then return to normal.

If the elevator is going *down,* rise to your toes as the elevator starts to move, and gradually lower your heels as the elevator continues to move. When the elevator stops at the bottom, momentarily sink in your knees a little. (Do the same little "bump" movement for each time the elevator stops on the way to your floor, too.)

When the elevator stops on your floor, watch the doors open, and walk out of the elevator.

The elevator illusion can also be used as a group exercise. Different people can get on or off at different floors, for instance, or the elevator can get stuck between floors. Use your imagination. The challenging part of the group exercise is coordinating the "bumps." Make sure that the entire group moves together, in the same direction, at the same time.

DO'S AND DON'TS

- *Do* remember to "bump." *Don't* just stand there. React to the movement of the elevator car, and do something interesting while the car is moving.
- *Do* "set the stage." *Don't* just walk into the elevator and start "bumping." The audience will have no idea what you're doing.
- *Do* try to act realistically in the elevator. *Don't* overstate your environment by feeling along the walls on the inside of the elevator car. The audience will go with you on this illusion without much extra guidance. Most of them have been on an elevator at some time in their life, and they have a good sense of the dimensions of the elevator car, the size of the doors, and so on. You don't have to spell it out.

Exercises

JOB INTERVIEW (SOLO EXERCISE)

This is an opportunity to use many of the illusions that you've learned—*objects, walking, going up and down stairs,* and *riding an elevator*—in a single exercise.

A single performer, the applicant, walks slowly onstage, reading the classified section of the newspaper, looking for a job. Applicant circles a few ads in the paper, finds a suitable ad to answer, and sets off.

Applicant begins walking down the street, checking the addresses of the office buildings along the way, looking for one particular address. Applicant stops in front of the right address, checks it against the ad in the paper, tucks the newspaper under an arm, and enters the building. (Applicant may walk up an exterior stairway and enter the building through a pushbar door or a revolving door.)

Applicant inquires at the information desk in the lobby of the building and is directed upstairs. Applicant goes up the first flight of stairs and at the top of the stairs proceeds down a corridor to an office door.

Applicant knocks, waits for a response, and enters. At the reception desk, the applicant inquires about the ad in the paper and is told to try the next floor up. Applicant exits the office, goes back down the corridor to the stairs, climbs the stairs to the next floor, repeats the office business, and is directed to yet another office on the next floor.

Once again the applicant leaves the office and goes up to the next floor. Again the same business. Tired and sweaty, the applicant reaches the right office, and is ushered in for an interview.

From here, the performer can decide on the course of the interview, and whether or not the job is successfully obtained.

Applicant leaves the interview and walks back down the corridor to the stairs. Rather than going all the way back down on foot, the applicant rings for the nearby elevator and rides back down to the lobby.

Applicant gets out of the elevator, leaves the building, walks back onto the street, and walks off the stage.

An interesting aspect of this exercise is that by using all the available illusions, it is possible to perform the whole piece in the space of only a few square feet.

UPS AND DOWNS (SOLO EXERCISE)

In this exercise, you learn how to show stairs, escalators, elevators, and other illusions by moving behind a "flat." (A flat is a standard piece of theatrical scenery, generally made of muslin fabric stretched over a wooden frame, which is then painted to suit its intended use.) For this particular exercise, a flat about three and a half feet high by about eight or nine feet long (with some sort of brace to hold it upright on its side) will work best.

Stairs ■ Starting at one end of the flat, take your first step "down" behind the flat in a slight bouncing motion. Keep your upper body *upright.* Continue down the stairs, bouncing a little lower with each step, until you have moved out of sight behind the flat, about halfway across it. Pause momentarily, turn, and come up the same stairs, using the same bouncing motion, or continue across the flat, going up a flight of stairs to the other side. Step back fully into view past the end of the flat on the last step.

Remember to keep your upper body straight, to do the slight bouncing motion with each step, and to keep the steps consistent, up and down.

Escalator ■ Start at one end of the flat. Step onto the escalator with a slight "bump" motion. When you first step onto the escalator, lean slightly backward, as the stairs move away from you. Instead of bouncing, as in the stairs, take long, slow, *gliding* steps forward, as your gradually lower your body behind the flat. You should be out of sight by about halfway across the flat. Pause momentarily in the center of the flat, and then either turn and retrace your steps or continue to the opposite end of the flat, riding the escalator back up. Take long, gliding steps, and gradually rise into view.

When you get ready to step off the escalator at the top, do another slight "bump," leaning forward a little as you come back to solid ground and slow down your momentum.

If you choose to use a railing with the escalator, remember that it travels *with* you, not in sections like it would on a stairway. You can also grasp the moving railing first, then let it pull you into the illusion.

Again, it is important that your upper body stays upright, and that your steps are very smooth and controlled.

Elevator ■ The elevator is most effective if you come up from behind the flat *after* going down the stairs or riding down the escalator.

Prepare yourself for the elevator by taking a position with your feet a little farther than shoulder width apart, in a deep knee-bend. Straighten your legs, with your upper body straight, and come up slowly from behind the flat. To go back down, push the elevator button and slowly bend your knees until you are again out of sight behind the flat.

Moving Sidewalk ■ Step onto the moving sidewalk, with a little "bump," at the end of the flat. Take slow, gliding steps to move your body along the length of the flat to the other end. Step off, again with a little "bump."

Your upper body remains in view. Remember to glide along smoothly. The audience should see no perceptible movement of your legs or feet.

With the moving sidewalk, the escalator, or the elevator, you can change direction at any time by simply adding a little "bump," and going off in a different direction. You can go forward, backward, sideways, or in circles.

When performed correctly, the illusions in Ups and Downs are very effective. An audience will almost believe that there is a hole in the floor in the stairs, escalator, and elevator illusions, and that the floor is actually moving in the moving sidewalk illusion.

Performance Piece

UPS AND DOWNS

You can use the illusions in the Ups and Downs exercise, and others of your own devising, to create a very effective performance piece. The piece can feature as many people as can practicably move or fit behind the flat. It could begin with an exploration of the four basic illusions—stairs, escalator, elevator, and moving sidewalk—by one person at a time, then move on to variations and combinations of these illusions.

To end the performance piece, you or the group can simply go down the stairs, escalator, or elevator, never to return, as the lights fade. Or one person could come back up in the elevator and walk off-stage, pulling the flat off as everyone else scurries along behind it hidden from view.

If they are working close to a back curtain, the performers can slip through the curtain (being careful not to move it) as they finish, until everyone is gone. If the flat has been rigged so that it can be collapsed from offstage, the audience will be very surprised to see that everyone has disappeared.

This kind of piece is particularly effective at the end of a mime program. It lets the audience relax and have fun and use their imagination almost effortlessly. A solo piece of about five or six minutes should be sufficient. A group piece should be a few minutes longer. If the performance piece is too much longer than that, the audience will lose interest, and the effects of the surprising juxtaposition of illusions will be lost. Leave the audience wanting more, always the best way to leave them.

Some possible variations of the Ups and Downs performance piece are:

The Chase ■ People chase one another, downstairs and up, up and down the escalator, in side-by-side elevators, back and forth on the moving sidewalk.

The Fight ■ The combatants start a fight in view of the audience, and gradually slip out of view behind the flat. Arms and legs and heads appear flying through the air above the flat. Perhaps a whole body, self-propelled or tossed by a group, might even sail by.

The Shooting Gallery ■ One performer steps out in front of the flat with a gun, while others move back and forth behind the flat in shooting gallery fashion, reacting appropriately if they're hit, and otherwise going back and forth.

HELPFUL HINTS

Set up the flat so that the audience cannot see around the ends. If one or more people have to stay behind the flat for any amount of time, they can simply slide upstage, away from the flat, to make room for the others. They will not be seen by the audience if they stay in the center of the flat area.

Different illusions can easily be performed at the same time. You will need to experiment to determine which ones work best together, but you are not as limited as you would be without the flat. The flat seems to facilitate combining illusions because it relieves the audience of having to watch anything more than your upper body. It helps them "see" what might require a little more effort on their part under the normal circumstances of a mime performance.

Move quickly from one illusion to another. The illusions will seem more believable to the audience if your spend little or no time preparing them for what's to come. Surprise them with each new illusion or activity.

Don't stay too long out of sight behind the flat. In time, the audience may lose interest. Pause only momentarily to change directions, to change illusions, or simply to catch your breath.

These illusions are physically demanding (as you will soon find out), and they require diligent, conscientious practice and rehearsal to be most effective.

Slow Motion

Slow motion is not an illusion as such. It is a *technique,* or skill, not an illusion. The technique of slow motion *does* manipulate the three elements of time, space, and energy, but it does not require any particular level of *imaginative response* from the audience, as many of the other illusions we've talked about do. As a technique, it can be used *with* other illusions, of course, and is very interesting to watch when done well, but the audience only has to *watch* the slow motion, simply *perceive* it, not *process* it in their imagination.

Slow motion requires considerable physical control and skill. It is essential to know what every part of your body is doing, and how all the parts of your body work together. As with all the other mime illusions, the laws of nature are still in effect; the only difference is they work slower. In walking in slow motion, as in the walking illusion, you must supply the movement that is ordinarily supplied by your momentum and the natural movement of your body.

One of the most important aspects of slow motion is the controlled *transfer of weight,* The transfer of weight must take place at the same speed and in the same rhythm as your other motions. This requires a good deal of balance and coordination, but most of all it requires considerable concentration. Walking in slow motion requires not only that your arms, legs, and head move slowly, but that the transfer of weight from one leg to another also occurs slowly and smoothly, with no noticeable break in the movement.

Another consideration is that, contrary to how it may appear, all the parts of your body do *not* move at the same speed in slow motion. If they did, your movements would look very mechanical, like a robot. Practice moving in a normal, natural way, but with all your movements slowed down. The parts of your body must move in "relative" slow motion. Your movements in slow motion may not necessarily *feel* natural, but they must nevertheless *look* natural to the audience.

While you practice moving in slow motion, also be aware of the small parts of your body—your fingers, eyes, and toes. In sitting down, for instance, your hands and fingers should take the weight of your body gradually and smoothly. You should also blink your eyes in slow motion, and move them slowly when you look from place to place. Again, this will all require a great deal of concentration to ensure that you are in *total* control of every part of your body.

Space Walk and Underwater

Being able to move in slow motion will help you learn two other illusions—*space walk* and *underwater.* These two illusions are related, but not identical. Both require well-controlled movements to define the illusions clearly for the audience. Although it is possible to make fast movements in space and underwater, it is best to keep the movements relatively slow and controlled to best define the illusion.

The major difference between moving in space and moving underwater is a matter of *resistance.* In space there is no resistance to your movements—if you raise your arm, it will keep moving until you stop it. Underwater, however, there is resistance to your movements. You must move your arm against the resistance of the water, and your arm will gradually stop moving unless you continue to exert the energy necessary to keep it moving. This principle of resistance applies no matter what the movement may be. In space, there is *no* resistance. Underwater, there *is* resistance.

With respect to these two illusions, there is also the problem of breathing, something that doesn't really apply to any other illusions. It is generally assumed by the modern audience that you will be wearing some sort of space suit or other self-contained life-support system in space, or that you are moving in a life-supporting environment, like a space station or shuttle. If you make it a point to put on your space suit, the audience will accept that you can breathe naturally and normally, and probably will no longer think about it.

Underwater, however, you must take the time to clearly define your manner of breathing or of not breathing. You can define a snorkel or scuba gear, or you can simply hold your breath. Realize, however, that if you *do* choose to hold your breath underwater, you must come up for air periodically, if for no other reason than to give the more empathetic members of the audience a chance to breathe, too. Some members of your audience will hold their breath, sometimes without even realizing it, while you are performing your underwater movements.

The space walk illusion requires nothing more than an awareness of the lack of resistance to movement mentioned above. When you move in space, let your arms and legs "float" whenever they are not actively involved in movement. Stay relaxed. Stay light on your feet. Keep all your joints flexible and loose, and move quietly and easily.

For the underwater illusion you can choose between two techniques. The first involves simply moving in a natural way, trying to duplicate as best you can the way you move when you're in the water. Simply move a little more slowly and fluidly than you would normally. Remember that there will be a slight resistance to your movements. You should exert a little more energy to get a movement going than if you were standing in the air, and let any movement that is not sustained come to a stop. There should be a floating sensation in your movements, but the floating should be balanced with the natural resistance of the water.

Keep your feet slightly apart. Try to distort your body parts just a little, if you can, to show the diffraction of light through water.

The second underwater technique is a more stylized interpretation of underwater movement, somewhat like the stylized running illusion is for the running motion. Once in the water, by whatever means you can devise, keep one foot firmly on the floor. Whatever movements you make should flow from there. A positive aspect of the stylized underwater technique is that you can more easily show upward and downward movement through the water than you can with the more realistic underwater technique. You can also show swimming movement much more effectively.

Final Notes on Illusions

Illusions are a distinguishing aspect of the art of mime. They are or can be the technical foundation of many mime performances. Illusions can form the basis for a complete performance piece. It takes just a little imagination to transform walls into a box, and then to use the box as the jumping-off point or central idea for a performance piece.

Illusions should not be the *entire* focus of a performance, however. Illusions should appear as a natural extension of the performance, should be totally integrated into the performance, and should not draw undue attention away from the overall presentation. Nor should they draw attention to themselves unnecessarily. The art of mime is based on *all* the elements of performing art—ideas, thoughts, and feelings expressed through character and situation—not simply on the technical expertise of the performer. Technique *and* expression work together in mime, as in any other art. Good mime performers don't need to show off their technical skills. Their overall performance "speaks" for itself.

Illusions fulfill a very practical as well as imaginative purpose. Through illusions you can create your own environment and move from place to place, even cover great distances, with relative ease. You are not limited to the "real" world, by the dimensions of a stage or its scenic capabilities. You are free to define your performance environment any way you choose, without restriction, and you are free to *change* it at will.

Technically speaking, though, illusions are not *exactly* what happens if you were actually to perform a particular activity. Illusions are designed to *appear* real. The illusions of walking or of riding a bicycle are only approximations of the actual movements involved. They require that the audience supply what's missing with their imagination, another distinctive aspect of the art of mime.

Experienced performers use illusions sparingly and instinctively, moving in and out of illusions almost imperceptibly. The illusion of walking, for instance, need not be used unless it is really necessary or central to your performance. For example, if the distance you need to travel can be covered within the actual performance space, then simply walk there. Repeated illusory walking for short distances will only confuse the audience. Illusions should appear as a natural extension of your performance. You should be able to move smoothly and seamlessly from real to imaginary. There should be no apparent break between reality and illusion that would cause the audience to have to switch mental gears just to keep up with you. Your use of illusions should not detract or distract from your overall performance.

By now you have learned a number of illusions and mime techniques that you can use to improvise solo and group exercises and to develop your own original performance pieces. There is no limit to what you can do in mime with the application of just a little creative energy, imagination, and conscientious practice.

Characterization | 7

The most essential point to remember about characterization and about building a character is that every character must be approached as a living, growing human being with thoughts, feelings, and emotions. Furthermore, every character is *unique,* if for no other reason than no two performers will portray a character in precisely the same way. Just as every person alive is unique, each character you portray should also be unique.

Lack of the spoken word should not seriously impair the ability of the mime performer to develop even the most complex characterization. The mime must, however, define the character in movement and gesture alone. Every movement that a character makes is a capsulized statement, a condensed version, of that character's *entire* personality. Every character's inner and outer qualities are revealed through action, and each action reflects the character as a whole. Every movement that you make reflects your personality. The same holds true for every character you portray.

Levels of Characterization

There are four basic levels of characterization through which a complete character develops.

PHYSICAL

This level includes anything that can be applied directly to the character's overall physical appearance and physical capabilities. What does the character look like? What is the character's age? sex? build? general physical attitude and potential? Is the character young or old? robust or sickly? tall or short?

ENVIRONMENTAL

A character is a reflection of his or her environment in the same way that you are a reflection of yours. A character is not an individual isolated in space but exists within a certain time and place, a *particular* environment. Where has this character come from? What is the character's occupation? social status? educational level? How does the character relate to his or her environment?

PSYCHOLOGICAL

How does the character think? What makes this character tick? How would the character react to a particular situation? How does the character respond, intellectually, to his environment? What does the character think of himself?

EMOTIONAL

The emotional qualities of a character are based, to some extent, on the psychological aspects of the character. The emotional level reflects how the character makes judgments and choices. How does the character resolve conflicts and problems? What are the character's standards of behavior, for herself and for others? What is the basis of her sense of right and wrong? Is the character outgoing or reserved? friendly, cautious, or hostile? loving or self-centered?

All of these levels work *together* to form a complete, well-rounded, well-defined character, and each level helps the audience understand a character more fully. A certain character may appear physically weak, for instance, and this may be the result of an emotional problem rather than a physical defect. Another character may appear strong despite physical shortcomings because he has a positive, outgoing, friendly outlook on life, and projects his sense of well-being through his actions.

In mime, characters can only be portrayed in terms of physical action. As mentioned previously, in mime there is only "show"—no "tell." You can't stop to explain things about the character to the audience. Anything that an audience learns about a character they learn only from what a character does, and how she does it. The audience will understand intuitively what a character is thinking, based on their own life experience and their own understanding of human nature.

Be aware that except for purely involuntary reactions to unexpected circumstances, a character cannot perform an action without first having a thought. Action always follows thought, no matter how fleeting that thought may be. The thought must come first. The action reflects the thought and, by extension, reflects the character of the individual as a whole.

Types of Action

There are four basic types of action to consider.

CHARACTER ACTIONS

These are related to the purely physical attributes of the character, and the actions that help to show these particular qualities—age, strength, size and shape, physical condition.

PRIMARY ACTIONS

Any movement *necessary* to perform a particular physical activity is a primary action. The physical activities of standing up, sitting down, walking across a room, closing a door, are examples of primary actions. These are basic actions, without embellishment. Primary actions are what the character does. Primary actions are the building blocks of physical characterization. They are the essential movements through which character is first revealed.

SECONDARY ACTIONS

Secondary actions are how the character performs a primary action. These actions are movement added to a primary action, an embellishment of a primary action. Any movement that accompanies a primary action but that is not absolutely necessary or essential to the activity is a secondary action. These are actions used not to accomplish a specific task but to *heighten* the effect of a primary action and to express a particular attitude or emotional frame of reference. Closing a door is a primary action. Slamming the door out of frustration is a secondary action. The door does not need to be slammed for it to be closed. Slamming the door is an addition to the action of closing the door that reveals an aspect of the character who is doing the slamming. Walking across a room is another primary action. *How* the character walks across the room is an example of a secondary action that helps reveal the character through movement. Secondary actions are very important in defining a character. They give a character depth and impart substantial meaning to the character's actions.

ACTIONS OF REACTION

As far as the character is concerned, this type of action is actually an *involuntary* reaction to another action or event. Reactions to heat or cold, pain, or a sudden or unexpected action by another character fall into this category, as well as any unprepared emotional reaction. Any physical response by a character to the environment that is not a purposeful or conscious movement is an action of reaction. It is important to note that characters have actions of reaction, but performers don't. Every movement that a performer makes on stage is (or *should* be) a conscious effort, a purposeful and controlled activity intended to contribute to the action of the piece and to reveal the character being portrayed. Characters may react without thinking, but performers must act and *appear to react* on purpose.

It is important to view each character as part of the whole performance picture *and* as an individual. Each character exists in two frames of reference: (1) in the external environment in which the character lives and (2) in the character's own thoughts, feelings, and ideas. These two elements of characterization work closely together, as they do in real life, and each must be clearly defined for the audience.

The *external* environment, the world in which the character lives, is defined through illusions, objects, and situations that the audience perceives *in their imagination.* As mentioned previously, the *internal* personality of the character is revealed through actions that occur *within the external environment.* These actions are not imaginary, but *real* and *immediate.* The audience sees what is actually happening.

Every character *wants* something. The obstacles that arise in the character's environment create the *conflict,* the struggle that the character has to undertake to get what he or she wants. The character's struggle to overcome the obstacles provides the story line, or plot, of the piece. Because of this struggle to get what they want, characters must *change* through the course of a performance piece. That's what makes them interesting. The character goes through a transformation from the beginning of the piece to the end, a purposeful journey of discovery and resulting change that holds the audience's attention and causes them to think about what they see and to empathize with the character. The character *and* the struggle must be interesting to an audience to hold their attention.

Building a Character

There are a number of schools of thought about and methods of building a character. One method works from the physical level to the emotional level, by first analyzing the physical details of the character and then fitting all the pieces together. The performer hopes to bring the character to life by evoking certain emotional feelings through physical activity.

A second approach is to determine the emotional state of the character and to let the physical activity of the character flow from and reflect the character's emotional responses to his or her environment. One other method is to imagine the character as completely as possible, physically and emotionally, then integrate the performer's own abilities into that characterization.

The first two methods are like paintings that appear a little at a time, color by color, until the completed image appears. The third method is like a paint-by-number painting—the outline appears first and is then filled in with the colors at hand, in the best possible way, trying to stay inside the lines.

Each performer approaches each character differently, of course, and the method used to build a character will vary with each performer as well. A character seems to develop most fully, however, when the approach is not limited to any one particular method. The objective for the performer is a well-balanced characterization. Since a character develops from both physical *and* emotional qualities, perhaps a combination of methods that also considers the performer's own abilities would be the best approach. This balanced approach avoids the shallow clichés evident in a purely physical approach (shaky old people) and the emotional sterility that can arise from the purely intellectual approach (mechanical men).

No matter which approach or method is used, the *overall* objective in developing a character is to make the character *believable.* This is the most important aspect of *any* characterization. The performer and the audience must firmly believe that this character is a living being, a truly unique and interesting individual.

In addition to bringing the character to life, the mime must also provide the physical environment, situations, and circumstances for the character. In building a character and projecting that character onstage, each mime performer is expected to utilize all of his or her available energy and resources. Performers may never come in contact with every type of character they may be called upon to portray, but they can fashion an entirely acceptable characterization from elements of the many different people with whom they share their existence. A substantial part of every character is what the performer remembers, has experienced physically, intellectually, and emotionally. All aspects of the performer's memory, existence, and imagination must work together to impart an inner reality—a *believability*—to each character.

The next chapter offers several ideas for approaching characterization in terms of performance pieces. The exercises will help you integrate characterization with the mime skills that you've already developed.

Developing Original Material 8

*M*ost mime performance pieces arise from improvisation. You begin with an idea, an image, a technique or illusion, an interesting character, or even just a feeling, and you work with that initial concept. You explore it and experiment with it. In time, a story starts to take shape. Characters develop. The main idea, the theme, begins to expand. The piece starts to grow, and soon it takes on a life of its own. It seems as if the piece is telling *you* what to do. Don't be alarmed. This is the way it *should* be. When the piece starts taking on a life of its own, then you've *got* something—potential. It's the beginning of the next great mime performance piece.

Mime shares with other performing arts a number of basic structural elements from which an effective performance piece evolves. Mime, like any other form of dramatic expression, is a representation of man, or woman, in action. The action of mime is the movement that forms the framework for the development of the character(s) and theme of the piece.

First of all, a mime piece must have a *plot*—a story. It must have *characters* (at least one). It must have a *theme,* or central idea. Plot, character, and theme are the three essential elements of any dramatic presentation. A mime piece without a plot is lifeless. Nothing happens. A piece without a character doesn't exist, since in mime the character is the physical embodiment of the piece. Without a theme, without a motivating force, without an inner life, the piece is nothing more than physical exercise.

Plot

The *plot,* the story of the piece, must have a beginning, a middle, and an end. This may seem overly simplistic, but you must decide how and when to take up the action of a piece, what to do to develop it, and when and how to end the piece for the greatest dramatic effect and for the greatest possible emotional impact on the audience.

The beginning of a mime piece is not necessarily where an action begins, but where the action of the piece is taken up. This may seem a contradiction in terms. By way of explanation: Characters in a dramatic presentation are coming from somewhere, but it is not always necessary to show where, exactly, it is they're coming from. A character enters a room, for example. Is it necessary to show that character walking down the hall to the door to that room? Is it necessary to go back even further to when that person entered the building before walking down the hall to the door to enter the room? To take this example to its extreme, is it necessary to go all the way back to show this character getting up in the morning, getting dressed, having breakfast, and so on? Probably not. If it *is* important to show that activity, then *that's* where the piece should begin. Otherwise, take up the action at a point close to where the interest of the piece lies, where the most relevant activities of the character take place. There is only one best place to begin the piece. It may take a considerable amount of time and effort to determine where, exactly, that place is, but the results will be well worth the effort.

In the opening moments of a piece, you provide everything the audience needs to know to understand the *rest* of the piece. In theatrical terms, this is the *exposition.* The exposition introduces the characters, establishes the setting or environment for the piece, and begins to develop the theme. There may be surprises along the way, of course, but they will only be surprises if the information and the environment for the surprise has been well established beforehand. A sudden turn of events requires that there first be events to turn.

The middle is where the piece develops, where the characters, the environment, and the situations of the piece are expanded and explored. The middle of the piece contains the problems, or *complications,* that arise for the characters, the inherent *conflict* that occurs because of these complications, and the ultimate *climax,* or high point of the piece. All of this is based on what has gone before, in the exposition. The middle of the piece furthers the action, further develops the theme, and carries the piece along to a logical, believable conclusion.

As a point of reference, there are basically three types of theatrical conflict:

1. *Man/woman against man/woman.* A character wants something. Another character wants something else. The conflict develops as each character pursues his or her own goals or objectives. It's a fight, a struggle for domination of one character over another. To be interesting for an audience, though, it needs to be a fair fight between evenly matched opponents. The outcome of the struggle should not be apparent to the audience until the climax. If it is too obvious from the start which character will prevail, the audience will lose interest.

2. *Man/woman against nature.* Nature, in this case, can refer to any number of elements in the character's environment—physical laws, a deity, the physical world, or some other external force outside the character's control—with which the character is in conflict. The simplest illustration is the illusion of walking against the wind. The character struggles to overcome a natural force, the wind. The interest for the audience lies not so much in the physical illusion but in the struggle. The character strives to conquer the wind, is pushed back repeatedly, yet somehow manages to prevail in the end through strength of character and strength of will (or simply strength of legs).

3. *Man/woman against himself/herself.* This can take the form of a moral, ethical, or psychological dilemma. The character must solve a problem that arises from within. It is a conflict of the character's own making. Given two courses of action, which will the character choose? The interest for the audience lies in how the character goes about solving the problem, and in what the character (and the audience) learn from the experience.

The end of a piece resolves any conflict(s), solves any remaining problem(s), and brings the piece to a close. The *resolution* of the piece should tie up any and all loose ends (certainly the crucial ones), and should provide a satisfactory and believable conclusion.

It's also important to remember that "it's over when it's over." (No need to wait for the fat lady to sing.) When you have "said" all that you have to say, and said it as well as you can, then stop. End the piece. There is nothing to be gained by drawing the piece out simply to hammer your theme home to your audience. If you present your theme clearly and effectively, the audience will get it. Trust yourself, and trust the audience. The audience is not your adversary. You and they are in this together. Work *with* them. Invite them into your world, help them along, and they will go with you to the ends of their imagination.

The plot encompasses not only what happens, but also where and when the action of the piece takes place—the setting. In developing original pieces, be sure to consider the setting, as well as the other essential action elements of the plot. You will create the setting by defining imaginary objects and utilizing the various mime illusions.

It is also possible to define the when of a piece, but actual time will likely be somewhat indistinct. It is a limitation of the art of mime that time is difficult, sometimes impossible, to define clearly for the audience. "Waking up in the morning," or "going to sleep at night" are only general indications. Often, that level of specificity will be the best you can expect. Luckily, a precise time is rarely crucial to the audience's perception or understanding of a mime piece. When a specific time is essential to a piece, it is usually indicated by costuming or perhaps by a program note.

Characters

The essentials of characterization have already been discussed in Chapter 7. Remember that the character is going on a journey from the beginning of the piece to the end. Whatever is encountered along the way forms the basis for the *plot,* the essential action of the piece, which in turn is based on the *theme*.

Theme

Every mime piece should have a central *theme* or idea, the reason the piece exists. Basically, this is what the piece *means,* what gives the piece its inner life and what you want the audience to understand about it. This theme need not be particularly complex or profound. It could be quite simple, even silly. The important thing to remember about the theme is that all the action of the piece, everything that your characters do, revolves around this central idea.

The theme is the bottom line of the piece. It is the sole reason that the plot and characters exist. All the elements of the piece, every action that takes place, every character that appears, every illusion that is performed, must somehow enhance the theme and contribute to it. Quite simply, if whatever you're doing doesn't contribute to the bottom line, then it shouldn't be there. A mime piece is most effective and most expressive when all that happens, every part of the performance, is relevant and appropriate to the theme. Don't do anything more than you absolutely have to do to convey the essence of the plot, character, and theme of your performance to the audience. Let them fill in the rest. Quite frankly, they will do it much better than you could. Remember that the audience will believe what they *think* they see, in their imagination, even more than what they actually observe. They will imagine far more of your performance if you guide them with a carefully constructed outline rather than spell it out in great detail.

A Brief Review

Every mime piece must have:

1. *Plot*—The action of the piece. The beginning, middle, and end. In more precise theatrical terms: exposition, complications, conflict, climax, resolution. The what, where, and when.
2. *Characters*—The who. Unique, believable, consistent. All their actions are motivated, relative to the theme.
3. *Theme*—The bottom line. The why. The inner life of the piece. The underlying reason that everything happens.

A mime piece can develop from any one of these three basic elements. It is not necessary, for instance, to always start with a theme, although you will need one somewhere along the way as your piece develops. Perhaps a certain kind of conflict appeals to you. You imagine characters involved in that conflict. A story starts to take shape in your mind. From the conflict, and the characters, and the story, a theme starts to evolve.

There are two types of mime pieces: *literal* and *abstract.* A literal mime is a fairly straightforward, uncomplicated interpretation of the real world—objects, characters, situations. In this type of mime, plot or character is of primary importance. The piece develops within the standard form—exposition, complications, conflict, climax, resolution—and when it's over, it's over. End of story.

An abstract mime relies on symbolic movement, symbolic references, and intuitive responses from the audience, and invariably raises sometimes ambiguous questions about the human condition that linger long after the piece has ended. The performer's intent is to cause the audience to think, to ponder, to investigate, to question a particular aspect of their existence. The plot and characters of an abstract piece are wholly secondary to the theme. The dramatic elements of the piece may not fall neatly into the standard form. In fact, the plot and character(s) may be somewhat ambiguous as well. Nevertheless, the movement in an abstract mime must be as clear as in a literal piece, and the symbolic references should be accessible to the audience.

Illusions are used in both types of mime pieces, although a literal piece is more likely to use mime illusions in the actual presentation. It is interesting to note, however, that an abstract piece is likely to invoke a higher degree of imaginative response from the audience than a literal one. The imaginative response to a literal mime is generally limited to discerning the activities and environment of the characters—where the characters are, and what they're doing. In an abstract mime, the imaginative response will more likely focus on discovering the meaning behind the piece and in discerning the implications of the theme and its relevance to the life of the particular audience member.

An abstract mime is much more *personal* than a literal mime. It reaches more deeply into the minds of the audience members, and elicits a much more thoughtful and often more emotional response. Literal pieces expand the imagination. Abstract pieces expand awareness, understanding, and inner life—performer's and audience member's alike. Literal pieces are the bread and butter of mime. Abstract pieces are its heart, mind, and soul.

When you're working to develop original material, take whatever your imagination gives you, and work with that. Don't prejudge your ideas until you've given them time to develop. If you find yourself at an impasse with a piece, don't force it. Go on to something else. Come back to the piece later, with a more objective eye. Think about it. Analyze it. Try to discover where the problem lies. Use the three basic elements as a guide. Often, a piece is not working because it is deficient in one or more of these essential areas. The plot may be lacking an interesting conflict, or the characters may not be consistent and well motivated in their actions, or the theme may be unclear. Perhaps the piece is too literal or too abstract. Rework the piece. Try a new perspective or a slightly different emphasis. Some pieces arise full-blown out of an afternoon's improvisations. Other pieces take months or years to develop. Be patient. Persevere. Today's unfinished piece may be the beginning of tomorrow's masterpiece.

Improvisational Exercises

The following improvisational exercises are intended to help you expand your sense of awareness, coordination, creative abilities, and imagination and to help you develop ideas for performance pieces. Every piece begins with an idea. These improvisational exercises will give you a wider range of ideas from which to choose.

OBSERVATIONS (SOLO EXERCISE)

Take one day, a whole day, and simply *observe* the world around you. Find a place or places where you can sit, stand, or wander around observing people and what they do. Go to the mall or to a construction site or to the park. Watch not only what people *do* but *how* they do it.

You will notice, for instance, that people who are experienced and adept at what they do make their actions look effortless. There is a fluidity of movement and a focused energy that comes only with daily repetition and years of experience. You will discover insights into a person's character by watching how they approach and perform their activities. Sometimes you can even tell what people are thinking and their emotional state. It's not mental telepathy. What people think and feel is revealed through their bodies, through their movements and gestures. A person who is standing totally still and expressionless reveals nothing about herself. As soon as she begins to move, however, her body speaks volumes, particularly to practiced observers.

People watching is one of the greatest single activities you can do to help build your awareness of the world around you, your "character file," and your improvisational repertoire. Try to remember that mime is not simply an imaginatively based art. You need more than a great imagination to be a great mime. You need a tremendous awareness and understanding of your own environment and culture and a sensitivity to the many and varied cultures throughout the world.

Walk around in your own living environment, and touch the things, the *objects*. Touch every object. Lift it, if you can. Feel the size and weight. Feel the texture. Most of all, record in your mental "mime file" your physical reactions to everything you encounter. What, exactly, did you *do* when you picked up the object, felt it, moved it in your hands? Review the chapter on imaginary objects for other ideas and guidelines.

Observe the physical space, the *environment,* of the people and objects around you. How does the space affect what it is that people do? How do you and other people adapt to the space, the atmosphere, the overall environment in which you find yourselves? How does a confined space affect movement as opposed to a larger, open space? How does a sunny day affect physical activities and feelings as opposed to an overcast or stormy one? How would you re-create that environment or that particular physical atmosphere onstage? What would you do, physically, to convey that environment to the audience?

Every activity in mime takes place within an environment. You must be able to define each environment for the audience, as well and as clearly as you define any other aspect of your performance, and you can define that environment only through movement.

WHO, WHAT, WHERE (SOLO EXERCISE)

The performer is given a who, a what, and a where by the teacher/ leader or by other members of the group. The who is a *character.* The what is an *activity,* any activity. The where is the *location,* or the environment, of the activity.

The object of the exercise is somehow to relate in performance what often may be three totally unrelated things. Sometimes the who, what, and where will be totally absurd. No matter. That's your assignment.

Often, trying to relate three seemingly unrelated things can have a very positive and liberating effect on your creative powers. It can be a very mind- and creativity-expanding experience. Your imagination and creativity love a challenge. Take a minute or two to collect your thoughts, devise a plan of action, and jump in. Try to make as much sense of the who, what, and where as possible. You may surprise yourself.

Keep in mind when performing this exercise that there is no such thing as miming in general. As there is only acting in the specific, there is only miming in the specific. All the possible alternatives of movement must be carefully analyzed to determine the one particular and *specific* movement that most completely expresses your intentions.

When you choose or are assigned a location in the Who, What, Where exercise, for example, make it a *specific* location, as specific as possible. Don't be satisfied with "in a park" as your location. In *which* park? Take time to visualize that particular park, and be as specific as possible in defining that park environment for your audience. The greatest mimes, as well as the greatest actors, are very specific in their work. That's what makes them unique. And that's what makes them great. No miming in general. Be specific.

OBJECT, ILLUSION, CHARACTER (SOLO EXERCISE)

This exercise is much like Who, What, Where, but the elements are an imaginary *object,* one of the mime *illusions,* and a *character.*

The performer must somehow *integrate* the three givens into the improvisation. If, for example, the elements are a ball (object), climbing stairs (illusion), and a lawyer (character), the performer should not simply walk up the stairs as a lawyer, playing with a ball. He should try to weave these three elements into a cohesive story. It may be quite a challenge, at times, to make any sense of the three elements. If you've come this far in the book, however, you should be used to challenges, and welcome them. Simply do the best you can, and learn what you can from the experience.

Remember to be specific. Define a *specific* ball (not just any old ball), a *specific* set of stairs (not just any stairs), and a *specific* lawyer (not just any lawyer) engaged in *specific* activities in a *specific* environment. At times, you may not be able to define each of these elements as specifically as you would like. Stairs are stairs, for the most part, but the railing has some potential for specificity. Also, there is a specific way in which you (as the character) approach the stairs, a specific environment in which the stairs exist, a specific reason for the stairs' existence in this particular environment, and so on. If you specifically define everything *related* to the stairs, the stairs will often take care of themselves. The same principle applies to any other situation that may seem difficult or impossible to define in a specific way.

UPPING THE ANTE (SOLO EXERCISE)

It might prove very interesting to include one of the three types of conflicts discussed previously in this chapter as part of an improvisational exercise—who, what, where, plus *why*—the conflict of woman against nature, for instance. Or object, illusion, and character, plus the conflict of man against himself.

Taking it one step further, try to define not only the who, what, where, and why of an improvisation, but also the more elusive *when.* Some intriguing pieces might result from such an improvisational challenge.

Remember that an improvisation is not a finished, polished performance. Some days the ideas will flow easily, one right after another. Other days you will struggle to make sense of even the simplest suggestions. Some days you can do no wrong. Other days you will make mistakes, and it will seem like the improvisation just won't work. Try to take it all in stride. Right or wrong, success or failure, it's all valuable experience. You will learn as much from your mistakes as you will from your triumphs. Often you will learn more.

ADD-ON (GROUP EXERCISE)

One performer takes the stage and begins to mime an activity. The activity can be decided in advance or simply improvised. Other students "add-on" to the activity, one at a time (in a predetermined or random order), until all are involved.

At this point, you can simply end the activity, or performers can leave the stage in the same order that they joined the activity—first in, first out.

It's important in this exercise, as in all group exercises, that everyone works together on the same activity and doesn't go off on an individual activity, taking the focus away from the group.

IN AND OUT (GROUP ACTIVITY)

This exercise begins like the Add-On exercise above. The first performer begins an activity in mime, and a second joins in. At the time that the second performer joins in, however, the first person leaves the stage. The exercise continues in the same manner—as each new performer joins in, the other ceases the activity—until the activity will no longer sustain itself or until it is ended by the leader or group consensus.

A more challenging variation: As each new performer joins the activity, he or she begins a *new* activity, but one that might reasonably flow out of the old activity. This continues, with each new person devising a new activity as he or she joins in.

FREEZE AND FOLLOW (GROUP ACTIVITY)

One performer starts an activity. At some point in the activity, the performer should freeze, holding the position. (The performer can simply freeze on her own, or the leader can call out "Freeze.") A second performer assumes the same frozen position as the first performer. The first performer "unfreezes" and leaves the stage. The second performer "unfreezes" and continues the same activity or flows into a completely new one.

This exercise, like any of these group exercises and variations, can be continued *ad infinitum,* with people coming and going, even those who have been part of the same exercise previously. It's up to the group or the leader to decide when the exercise is over.

What Else?

What other exercises can you use to develop performance pieces? There is really no limit to what you can do in mime, so whatever you see, experience, or imagine can be the basis for a mime performance piece. Start with those activities that are most familiar to you, the things you do every day. Then try the activities you do *less* often but with which you are still familiar. Then simply venture further and further into your own imagination.

Look at the world around you, and re-create in mime the activities that you see. Every*thing* and every*one* in the world is fair game for mime. Study not only the activities around you but also the people. Watch their movements and their expressions. Observe their attitudes and their demeanor. How do they walk? How do they move? What is it about that person that makes him unique? Remember what people do, how they do it, and try to re-create it.

Finally, explore your dreams, your thoughts, your ideas, and your feelings. Try to decide how you can best express in mime those things about which you feel strongly. Mime is a very powerful medium of expression because it reaches *directly* into people's imagination. The images in mime reach into our *mind,* and they can also reach deep into our *emotions.*

Mime is not a mass-market art, nor does it necessarily appeal to the masses. Do not be misled or confused by the popular amusement-park and street-corner variety of so-called mime performers. Some may be gifted mimics or otherwise gifted entertainers, but what they do rarely reflects or constitutes the true *art* of mime. Examine what they do, and you will find that one or more of the essential elements of the art of mime is missing.

There may be no plot, for instance. In some cases, there may be no illusion. Mimicking the walk, movements, and gestures of passers-by, for example, is not illusion. It's just mimicry, no matter how skillful the performer may be. There may be no real communication between performer and audience, no cyclical flow of ideas, thoughts, or feelings. There may be little or no imaginative response from the audience. All that is required of the audience is that they observe. Most often, however, what is missing is a theme. Generally speaking, in this kind of performance there is no intrinsic, substantial meaning to the presentation. Mime illusions performed outside of a theme-based framework are nothing more than technical exercises, without meaning and often without artistry.

In this kind of performance, there is no bottom line other than to entertain. This is not to demean the work of the amusement-park and street-corner performers; to entertain is a noble calling in its own right. But none dare call it mime without first understanding the essential elements of the art of mime and being able to recognize these elements (or their absence) in the performance.

Unfortunately, it is this type of quasi-mime performance that has imparted a rather derogatory connotation to the terms "mime" and "mime artist," particularly for the general public. The mime that most people see, if they see any, is this "backyard" version—going for the easy laugh by mimicking passersby, making silly faces, annoying innocent patrons, taking pratfalls, and performing seemingly endless (and technically deficient) variations of "The Wall," "Blowing Up a Balloon," and "Walking Against the Wind"—a throwback to the popular variety entertainments of Greek and Roman mime. This all too common conception of "mime" has seriously undermined the public's understanding of the art of mime. As a result, the art of mime has most likely lost a considerable part of its potential audience. This is a challenge that every serious performing mime artist must understand, and strive to overcome.

Mime is an art of individuals, one to one, individual performer to individual audience member. Mime is a "direct access" art—direct access between you and the imagination of every individual member of your audience. You may have an audience of hundreds, even thousands, but you reach each member *individually,* one to one, person to person. There is nothing to come between you and the imagination, thoughts, and feelings of your audience. There are no words for the performer or the audience to hide behind in mime. There are no words to confuse people or to cause them to misunderstand or misinterpret what you're trying to express. Your audience may not even speak the same language you do, but they will understand what you are trying to show them. Decide what it is you want to show your audience, one to one, then determine the best way to show it.

In Performance 9

*M*akeup, costume, lights, sound, and the other technical elements of a theatrical performance are also important aspects of any mime presentation. Certainly, as a mime performer, you ought to be able to do without any or all of these things, relatively speaking. (A costume is advised, for decency's sake at least, and without lighting, the audience won't be able to see you. There's always sunlight, of course.) If you choose to use any of these things to enhance your performance, however, it is essential that you approach them with the same serious attitude and commitment with which you approach your mime artistry.

Makeup

One of the most personal aspects of mime performance is the performer's makeup. Each performer has his or her own way of applying the makeup and of giving it a personal touch that sets that performer apart from all others.

Mime makeup alone won't make you a mime, of course (no more than being able to do The Wall or The Tightrope), but makeup can enhance your performance in several ways. First of all, the makeup sets you apart as a performer. It gives you a sense of being different from "regular" people, and it imparts to the audience a sense that you, the performer, are "larger than life," someone interesting, someone worth watching. Makeup creates a slight emotional distance between you and your audience, and allows you increased access to their mind and imagination.

Makeup also enhances your physical projection—the audience can see your face better and can better see what your face is doing. (In a large or poorly lighted auditorium, this aspect alone is well worth the trouble it takes to put on the makeup.)

Instructions for applying the traditional whiteface mime makeup follow, the basic application steps as well as notes about stylizing or personalizing your makeup. Experiment with your makeup. Try different styles of foundation, eyes, and mouth. Add your own personal touches. The style you use may also depend to some extent on your performance situation. In a group piece, for example, you may wish all the performers to have a consistent style of makeup. For solo performances, a more personalized makeup may be more acceptable and appropriate.

WHAT YOU NEED

Listed below are the basics you'll need in your makeup kit (Illustration 19 is a photograph of an appropriately stocked makeup table). All these supplies can be readily acquired at any theatrical makeup supplier.

1. Foundation. White pancake makeup, applicator sponge (preferably real, not synthetic), and water; or clown white greasepaint. If you are using greasepaint, you will also need translucent powder, a powder puff, a powder brush, and theatrical makeup remover.
2. A black eyeliner or eyebrow pencil, and a pencil sharpener.
3. Red lip liner, and an eighth-inch lining brush. There are several different shades of red lip liner. Purchase two or three in the mid-to-dark range, but not the fire-engine-red variety.
4. Tissues.
5. A mirror, preferably one that is large enough to reflect your whole face at once.
6. (Optional) White masque makeup for blocking out your eyebrows.

FOUNDATION

There are two types of foundation makeup that work best for mime— dry cake makeup and clown white greasepaint. Cake makeup is quick and easy to apply, washes off with soap and water, and is relatively

Illustration 19. A well-stocked makeup table.

easy to touch up. Some performers find, however, that cake makeup isn't white enough and that it's sometimes difficult to cover dry or rough patches on your face effectively.

Clown white greasepaint takes longer to apply and is more difficult to remove, but the makeup is *very* white. Clown white also needs to be powdered, to set the makeup and prevent smears. Even with the powder, clown white can be difficult to maintain and touch up, particularly outdoors in the hot sun or under bright lights, and it can be uncomfortable to wear for prolonged periods of time. If you are allergic to makeup or have sensitive skin, clown white is not recommended. Cake makeup may have a tendency to dry out your skin with repeated or prolonged use, but it is not as likely to trigger an allergic reaction or cause your skin to break out. Try both, if you can, and decide for yourself which is more appropriate or acceptable to you.

Basic Application ■ Rub a damp sponge on the cake of makeup to pick up the color, then apply the makeup to your face. It is best to apply several light coats rather than one thick coat. If applied too heavily, the makeup may powder or flake.

There is no set procedure for where on your face to start applying the makeup. Simply wet the sponge, squeeze out most of the water, and apply the makeup any way you like. Cover your entire face to your hairline, in front of your ears, and down to your jaw line. (There is no need to put makeup on your neck or ears.) Try to cover your face evenly with the makeup, without smears or noticeable streaks. Remember that the audience will be considerably farther away from your face than you are from the mirror. The audience will never see the little flaws in your makeup, or in your face.

Apply clown white greasepaint with your fingers. First dot the greasepaint over your face with your fingertips. Wet your fingers with a little water, and spread the greasepaint evenly over your face. (The water helps the spreading—try it with and without water, and you'll see the difference.) At first you may find it difficult to cover your face evenly, without streaks, but with practice it can be done.

Stylizing Possibilities ■

- Using a black lining pencil, outline your face with a thin line. This will give the appearance of a mask, but a mask that is actually your own face.
- Instead of putting makeup all over your face, to your hairline and in front of your ears, apply foundation in an actual "mask" area, an oval, from the top middle of your forehead to your chin. Outline this mask with a thin black line, as above.

EYES AND EYEBROWS

Basic Application ■ Use a sharp, black eyeliner pencil. Line the upper edge of your eyelid from the inside corner of your eye to the outside corner. Outline your lower eyelid only from the inside edge of your iris to the outside corner of your eye. (Do not bring the two eyelid lines together at the corner of your eye, because doing so will make your eyes look smaller.)

If you have smallish eyes, or eyes that are close together, put the lines a little way from back from the edge of your eyelids. This will make your eyes appear larger and wider set.

Follow the line of your eyebrows with the black lining pencil. Correct for thick or thin eyebrows by using a relatively thinner or thicker line. Carry the pencil line of your eyebrows a little past the actual end of your eyebrows.

Stylizing Possibilities ■

- Extend the upper line out and up a little at the outer corner of your eyes, and take the lower line out and down. The added lines should be the same thickness as the original lines.
- Create "mime eyes." With the lining pencil, make a short, thick line on your lower eyelid, straight down from the center of your eye. You can make the same type of line at the outer corner of your eyes, or the thin line described above. The center line highlights the movement of your eyes.
- Cover your own eyebrows with clown white greasepaint or special white masque makeup, and then draw new, slightly arched eyebrows just above your own. (This may appear more mimelike, but it does somewhat restrict the expressiveness of your own eyebrows.)
- Experiment with stars, hearts, teardrops, rouged cheeks, and the like. Be warned, though, that this can easily become precious and cloying. In a controlled or otherwise serious environment, you may wish to forgo them.

MOUTH

Basic Application ■ With a liner brush, apply lip liner to your lips. You can compensate for what you may feel are any inadequacies by applying the liner slightly beyond or slightly within your own lip line. Blot the lip liner with a tissue to take off any excess, and to dull the shine.

Stylizing Possibility ■ Outline your lips with a thin, black line.

POWDER

If you use clown white greasepaint, once you have finished your foundation, eyes, and mouth, you will need to powder everything to set it. Use translucent (no-color) powder and a clean powder puff, lightly dusting your entire face. Check for shiny spots, and powder those areas again. With a soft powder brush, gently brush the excess powder off your face. (It is not necessary to powder cake makeup.)

REMOVING MAKEUP

Cake makeup can be removed easily with soap and water, or with any other makeup remover. Greasepaint must be removed with makeup remover, preferably one designed for removing theatrical makeup. Apply the makeup remover and tissue it off. There is also a theatrical makeup remover on the market that can be washed off with soap and water.

A WORD ABOUT HAIR

Your hair should be cut or styled so that it does not cover your face or obscure any of your features. Long, loose hair can be distracting to you and to your audience. Avoid eccentric hairstyles that distract or detract from your performance.

Costume

Because of the highly physical and energetic nature of mime, costumes for rehearsal and performance should be light, cool, strong, and comfortable. The material itself should be easy to care for, and crease-resistant if possible. Freedom of movement is important, of course, so performance costumes and rehearsal clothes should be fairly close-fitting, but not constricting or confining.

The audience has very little to look at other than your body, so your costume should be visually interesting and flattering, but not distracting. The standard-issue black-and-white costume is good for some mime pieces, but tends to become dull and uninteresting over time, particularly if used exclusively for an entire performance.

It is sometimes helpful to use a costume piece or two—a vest, tie, or skirt, for example—to suggest different costumes or characters. These kinds of additions should be used sparingly, however, and should not draw undue attention to themselves. A costume with just a little bit of character is preferable to a costume with absolutely no character at all.

There is a wide range and variety of ready-made dance rehearsal and performance clothes and costumes that are excellent for mime, including leotards of many different colors and styles, tights, and jazz pants. Jazz pants and leotards are appropriate for many mime performance styles and situations, indoors or out, and can be worn in many different and interesting color combinations. Tights are somewhat less flattering than jazz pants, since they draw attention to the legs, but they are perfectly appropriate and functional for rehearsal. One-piece jumpsuits and unitards are also available and can easily be worn with or without other costume pieces. Tights, jumpsuits, and unitards all require a fairly attractive and well-proportioned body inside them. Judge accordingly when choosing an appropriate costume for your performance.

The types of shoes available for mime include ballet slippers, jazz shoes, and specially made mime slippers (also known as "foot gloves"). The jazz shoes have a small heel and a flexible sole. Ballet slippers have a harder, less flexible sole that needs to be broken in. Mime slippers have no added hard sole or heel. They are generally sewn from one piece of leather and are very soft and flexible. They are the most practical shoes for mime, but may be much more difficult to find than ballet slippers or jazz shoes. Consult a theatrical footwear supplier for the type of shoes that best suit your performance situation and performance style.

Be sure to wear your performance costume in rehearsal at least two or three times before an actual performance, and be sure to break in your shoes long before your performance. It is always best to discover any shortcomings in your costumes (and thus be able to remedy them) *before* wearing them in front of an audience. You should also examine your costume closely before and after every performance for any necessary repairs.

All in all, your mime costumes should be carefully chosen. There is a wide selection available, so it should be relatively easy to find the type and style that best fits your performance needs. If all else fails, you can construct your costumes from scratch. Keep in mind, however, that your costume must be well built to withstand strenuous use, yet should be comfortable, versatile, and attractive.

Sets and Props

Ideally, you should use no sets or props in mime. Realistically, however, it may be necessary to use props that must remain consistent over a long period or that will be handled by several performers. If used, props should be simple. They should *suggest* an object, rather than *be* the object. One prop can serve a multitude of uses. A simple stick, for example, or any other basic artifact, can be used to represent many different objects. Overall, use props sparingly, and only when absolutely necessary.

Lights

Whenever possible, use area lighting, rather than a spotlight. The light from a spotlight is often very harsh and bright, and tends to flatten and wash out the performer. Pools of light are used to create area lighting. Small pools of light can be joined together to form larger pools.

Back lighting and side lighting should also be used whenever possible, particularly with whiteface; it will help keep you from looking flat and two-dimensional. Back and side lighting are also a simple way to achieve special effects. Use back lighting, for instance, for a silhouette effect, and use side lighting for more abstract, symbolic mood pieces.

Gel colors for the lights should reflect the mood of the performance piece. The lighting should not draw attention to itself, but support and enhance the performance. Subtle, controlled, and consistent lighting works best.

Also, try to develop a good light sense—the ability to find and stay in the light. It's a valuable performance skill. What does it matter what you do, or how well you do it, if the audience can't see you?

Sound

A mime performance should be able to stand on its own without any added sound. Music does help to set a mood, however, and can subtly enhance your performance, just as good costuming and lighting can. Sound effects—squeaky stairs, slamming doors, wind and rain—should not be used at all, of course. Let the audience "hear" the sounds of your performance in their own mind.

If you decide that music would enhance your performance, keep these points in mind:

1. Experiment with different types and styles of music. As a general principle, use simple, uncomplicated music—Bach instead of

Wagner, for example. Don't settle for music you know is not quite right. Your performance will suffer for it. Take the time to select just the right music. When in doubt, go without.

2. Mood, tempo, rhythm, and even instrumentation are important considerations in choosing your music. The music should be compatible with your performance in every way.

3. Be sure that your music is well recorded and well edited. Be aware of any extraneous sounds on the tape, like clicks, pops, and static. These kinds of sounds can be very distracting to the audience against the silence of your performance. Use good sound equipment to record the music and also to play it back for the performance.

4. Never trust your playback equipment (or any other electrical or mechanical object, for that matter). Electrical plugs get pulled. Fuses blow. Batteries go dead. Tapes break. Equipment can malfunction. Be prepared to do without.

The overriding consideration to remember in choosing music for your performance is that the music must support and enhance the mime. Mime is not performed *to* the music. (Mime performed to the music is dance.) The challenge is to find music that is interesting and enhances your performance, but does not dominate it or distract from it.

Performing Outdoors

It is likely that not all the performances in your lifetime will take place in a closed, controlled environment, like a theatre or auditorium. At times, you may be called upon to perform in uncontrolled environments—in parks, or on the street, or in malls or city squares. Some performers prefer the spontaneity and lighter atmosphere of this type of venue, while maintaining the integrity of the art of mime in their work.

The key to success, no matter the performance environment, is organization. When working outdoors or in other informal venues, keep the following guidelines in mind.

MAKEUP

Use cake makeup instead of greasepaint. Cake makeup is more comfortable, easier to touch up, and much easier to remove. Also, keep it simple. Your own face, with an individual distinguishing mark or two, will still set you off as a performer.

COSTUME

Your costumes should be light, cool, strong, colorful, and comfortable. Be creative, but remember that you may be spending many long, hot days in whatever it is you devise for you to wear. A brightly colored T-shirt, shorts or jazz pants with suspenders, and tennis shoes would do nicely. Add a vest, perhaps, or a hat. Your costumes should also be washable. If you get caught in the rain, your costume will be none the worse for it.

PACE

Keep your energy level high. Keep your show tight, and keep it moving. Make sure that all your material is well rehearsed. Don't just wander into the street and hope that everything works out. Improvisation in performance is not for amateurs.

Keep audience participation to a minimum. Some street performers are masters at drawing people out and getting them to contribute effectively. It's difficult to do this consistently, however. The participation of audience members can be very unpredictable. Often, audience participation will slow down the show. At other times, it can be disastrous.

MATERIAL

Use visually interesting, high-energy material. Literal mime pieces using a number of illusions work well. Overall, comic pieces will work best. Serious or abstract pieces will not fare well in an informal, uncontrolled environment. Much of your audience will be just passing by, and they will have no idea what you're doing if they don't watch the whole piece.

Vary your material. Build a stock repertoire of things you can do, and change your pieces around for each show, until you find the best possible combination in the best possible order. If you can juggle or do magic or acrobatics or ride a unicycle, add a short demonstration piece to your presentation. The variety will hold your audience's attention and interest. The nonmime activity will also help draw an audience.

The length of the show is up to you. This is the age of hard-hitting, flashy music videos, fast-moving video games, and short (sometimes *very* short) attention spans, so judge accordingly. A little experience will give you a good idea of how long you can work before people begin to lose interest. A good, tight, fifteen-to-twenty-minute high-energy show seems to work best. Anything much longer, and your audience will begin to wander away.

OTHER CONSIDERATIONS

Where to Perform ▪ Check out the local ordinances regarding public performances, and research possible venues in your area. It's very likely that some other performer will have already found the best spot to work. Keep looking. It's a big world out there.

What to Perform ▪ Observe other, more experienced performers. Learn from them. Watch how they work the crowd, and how they program their material. Also learn to be different from them.

Passing the Hat ▪ Passing the hat is a time-honored tradition among street performers. Avoiding the hat is a time-honored tradition among street audiences. Not everyone understands the convention of street performers passing the hat, so be sure to prime the pump with some coins and folding money. (You might even plant some friends or relatives in the audience with a little loose change.)

Put your "hat" somewhere near you on a box or on the ground so people can drop money in on their own, or pass through the crowd after your performance. Move quickly through the audience as they disperse. (Start toward the back of the crowd if you can, so they have to walk past you as they leave.)

Street Justice ▪ This is a general term meaning that anything can (and probably will) happen in an informal, uncontrolled setting like the street or a public park. Not all that happens will be to your liking, or to your benefit. The street is open to everybody, not all of whom will appreciate your efforts on their behalf. Expect to hear rude or otherwise unwelcome remarks about you and your show. Expect distractions and disruptions. Learn to accept these challenges as part of the environment. Keep it light. Have a good time.

Additional Performance Notes

As a mime performer, you must, like any other performer, respect the knowledge, capacity for understanding, and intelligence of your audience. You must not only be totally prepared, but enthusiastic and committed to the performance as well.

PROVIDE GOOD SURROUNDINGS

Be sure that your audience is comfortable. As best you can, eliminate or lessen distractions, particularly extraneous light and sound. The concentration and attention of the audience are very delicate. An audience can be very easily distracted. Give your audience every opportunity to stay with you every imaginary step of the way. The audience is your reason for being. Remember that they provide for you and your performance something you can't—an imaginative response. Without their imagination, you and your performance, being one and the same thing, simply don't exist. Treat your audience well.

START ON TIME

Make every effort to begin your performance when you've said you will and keep it running smoothly, without undue or unnecessary breaks or pauses. There is nothing as deadly to the continued interest and imaginative response of your audience than for them to sit out there in the dark, waiting . . . and waiting . . . and waiting for something, *anything,* to happen.

On a related subject . . . "The mind will not retain what the seat will not endure." If your show approaches ninety minutes or more in length, seriously consider an intermission. The audience will come back into the theatre after a short intermission refreshed and revived, their minds open to new challenges. Give yourself every opportunity to keep the audience receptive to your performance.

SHOW GOOD PERFORMANCE SENSE

Enter and exit the stage in character, and with good energy. Your characterization should begin offstage, well before your entrance, and should not end until you are well out of sight of the audience when you exit. "Stay in the scene," as stage directors say. Mistakes happen. Since you can't go back and undo them, ignore them and press on.

STAGE FRIGHT

Imagine that this is your very first mime performance. This may well be the first time you've ever appeared on stage, anytime, anywhere. You're scared to death. You're shaking all over. You don't think you can do it. You just know you're going to get out there in front of the audience and freeze solid. You want to run away, right now, and never, ever come back, but you can't, because you can't even move. It's time for your entrance. Oh, no. This is it. (You mumble a prayer to St. Jude, patron saint of hopeless causes.) You can't take it anymore. You're going to die!

But you don't. You walk out in front of that audience with an air of supreme self-confidence, as if you've done this a hundred times before, and you give an excellent performance. Of course, you can hardly remember it because you were scared to death, but you did it, and you did it well. There. Now you've had the experience. It's over. You're successful. How do you feel?

The human mind cannot distinguish between what is real and what is imagined. This principle applies equally to you as it does to your audience. If you imagine that you will fail miserably, then as far as your mind is concerned, you already have. If, on the other hand, you imagine that you will give an excellent performance, then in all likelihood you will. Try to visualize yourself doing well, and you've already done it!

In actuality, few people have died onstage, and it probably wasn't from stage fright. (According to tradition, Molière died onstage in performance, but he was suffering from exhaustion and a variety of other diseases, not from stage fright.) People manage, somehow, to go out there and give that first performance . . . and the next . . . and the next . . . and experience few ill effects from the experience (negative reviews notwithstanding).

You want to do well. You want to succeed, and perhaps even more important as far as your performance is concerned, your *audience* wants you to succeed, too. People don't go to the theatre hoping to be bored to death. They may well be, but generally speaking, your audience is expecting a positive, entertaining, fulfilling, perhaps even enlightening experience. They are ready and willing to meet you more than halfway, and they will forgive almost any mistake you make along the way *if* you believe in what you are doing, *if* you are committed to the performance, and *if* you are willing to expend your time and energy *with* them and *for* them.

What is commonly referred to as stage fright is really a combination of anxiety and anticipation. First of all, stage fright is not even a real fear. Fear itself is debilitating. You can't do anything. You can't move. You can't say anything. You can't even think clearly. Stage fright is based on self-consciousness, fear of failure, lack of experience, worry, nervousness, or any combination of the above.

Self-consciousness ■ First of all, the audience (except for your friends and relatives, of course) did not come to see you personally. They came to see what you can *do.* That should ease some pressure right from the start. The audience came to watch and experience the *whole* performance, not just your part of it. They came to be involved, and moved, and entertained. They didn't come just to see *you.*

Fear of Failure ▪ No performance has been or ever will be perfect. Something will go wrong with every performance, guaranteed. There is, however, no possible way for you to know, in advance, what that "something" will be. No use worrying about it. There's nothing you can do about it anyway.

Lack of Experience ▪ A reasonable anxiety. You don't know all there is to know about mime or performing. You probably never will. But that shouldn't keep you from trying. Think of each performance as part of a process, not necessarily as an end in itself. It's just a step along the way. Tomorrow you will be more experienced than you are today. And the next day you will be even more experienced than you will be tomorrow. You will learn by doing, but if you never do, you'll never learn. You've got to start somewhere. Might as well get this performance over with so you can get on with your life.

Worry ▪ Worry is a waste of time. Worry is nothing more than the misuse of your already overactive imagination—you imagine the worst thing that could possibly happen to you. Even if the worst *does* happen, which is not likely, worrying about it will make absolutely no difference at all.

Nervousness ▪ Nervousness is natural. Everybody gets nervous about something. For you, it may be this performance. You can help overcome your nervousness by channeling your excess energy into relaxation exercises or putting it into your performance. Overwhelm your audience with your energy and enthusiasm. They won't know what hit 'em. By the end of your performance they'll be standing on their feet, clapping their hands together, shouting "Encore! Encore!" It could happen.

Anticipation ▪ Anticipation is good. As a matter of fact, anticipation is great. Anticipation helps you get an edge and keep it. It helps raise your energy level, gets your heart pumping, and gets you ready to do great things. Deep inside, you know you're actually looking forward to your performance. You may be a little scared, you may not know quite what to expect out there, but you're ready, and that's what counts.

The Antidote ▪ The best antidote to stage fright ever devised is preparation. Imagine walking onstage as Hamlet without knowing your lines. There is no more horrible feeling than that overwhelming sense of fear and desperation. The better prepared you are, the less reason you will have to feel self-conscious, fearful of failing, worried, or nervous. Careful, conscientious preparation instills a strong sense of self-confidence and security in the performer. A sense of anticipation before a performance is good. Abject fear is not. To avoid fear, prepare.

An aside: The audience won't know you're nervous unless you tell them. You can take consolation from the fact that from their distance the audience can't see your quivering lip, your shaking knees, your trembling hands, or the knots in your stomach. (And since what the audience can't see in mime doesn't really exist, neither does your stage fright.) If you have prepared for this moment onstage, if you have trained your body and mind well, then you will be fine. Trust yourself. Relax. Enjoy the performance. You've got the best seat in the house.

The corollary to preparation is concentration. If you're paying attention to what you're doing, you won't have time to be nervous. Remain constantly aware of your surroundings, your movements, and the movements of the other performers. Stay in control of yourself at all times. Don't be distracted or dismayed by little things that are of no consequence to the overall performance. Keep your mind focused on what you're doing. The rest will take care of itself.

Respect the people with whom you work. This includes not only the other performers, but *everyone* involved with the performance— directors, producers, stage managers, technicians, stage crew, costumers, makeup crew, everyone. Remember that they have worked long and hard on this performance, too, and it is as important to *them* to have a good show as it is to *you*.

Final Words

The creative process involved in mime, or in any other art, has never been satisfactorily defined or explained. It is far too individualized a process to be analyzed objectively. In mime, the stimulation of the imagination is the very essence of the creative process. Elements of reality within our experience and environment must somehow be transformed or rearranged for the audience into an imaginative frame of reference.

The *intent* of the artist is also of primary importance. Without intent there is no art. The unique, expressive qualities of a work of art are achieved by the organization and *purposeful* articulation of its component parts. Each work of art is a consciously organized, developed, and unified relationship of all those parts, intended to project or evoke a sometimes specific, sometimes entirely abstract experience or response.

We naturally understand artistic expression best in terms of our own reaction to it. Art expresses and fulfills a basic, individual need. The underlying principle of artistic expression is an awareness and understanding of the human condition.

The art of mime relies on no material substance for its existence other than the artist. Through the artist, art is created, nurtured, and sustained. Henry Miller said, "A mime is a poet in action—he *is* the story he enacts." The mime *performer* is the mime *performance*, pure and simple. As a mime performer, you enact everything—characters, objects, props, set, illusions. To do this well demands a great deal of hard work and dedication on your part, but it can also reward you with a tremendous sense of accomplishment and an extraordinary means of personal and artistic expression.

Bibliography

Alberts, David. 1971. *Pantomime: Elements and Exercises.* Lawrence, KS: University Press of Kansas.

Avital, Samuel. 1977. *Le Centre du Silence Mime Workbook.* Venice, CA: Wisdom Garden Books.

Barlanghy, Istvan. 1967. *Mime: Training and Exercises.* Edited by Cyril Beaumont. London: Imperial Society of Teachers of Dancing.

Barrault, Jean-Louis. 1974. *Memories for Tomorrow.* Translated by Jonathan Griffin. New York: E. P. Dutton.

Carlson, Marvin. 1972. *The French Stage in the Nineteenth Century.* Metuchen, NJ: The Scarecrow Press.

Curtis, Paul. 1963. *The American Mime Theatre Textbook.* New York: American Mime Theatre.

Decroux, Étienne. 1985. *Words on Mime.* Translated by Mark Piper. Pomona, CA: Mime Journal.

Dorcy, Jean. 1961. *The Mime.* Translated by Robert Speller, Jr., and Pierre de Fontnouvelle. New York: Robert Speller and Sons.

Duchartre, Pierre Louis. 1966. *The Italian Comedy.* Translated by Randolph T. Weaver. New York: Dover.

Felner, Mira. 1985. *Apostles of Silence.* Rutherford, NJ: Farleigh Dickinson University Press.

Green, Martin, and John Swan. 1986. *The Triumph of Pierrot.* New York: Macmillan.

Hausbrandt, Andrzej. 1977. *Tomaszewski's Mime Theatre.* New York: Da Capo.

Kipnis, Claude. 1974. *The Mime Book.* New York: Harper & Row.

Littlewood, S. R. 1911. *The Story of Pierrot.* London: Herbert & Daniel.

Martin, Ben. 1978. *Marcel Marceau: Master of Mime.* New York: Paddington Press.

Nicoll, Allardyce. 1963. *Masks, Mimes, and Miracles.* New York: Cooper Square.

Oreglia, Giacomo. 1964. *The Commedia dell'Arte.* Translated by Lovett F. Edwards. New York: Hill & Wang.

Remy, Tristan. 1954. *Jean-Gaspard Deburau.* Paris: L'Arche Editeur.

Rolf, Bari, ed. 1980. *Mimes on Miming.* Los Angeles: Persona Books.

Shepard, Richmond. 1971. *Mime: The Technique of Silence.* New York: Drama Book Specialists.